THE CITY BY
THE ULTIMATE SAN FRANCISCO ITINERARY

SAN FRANCISCO

— TRAVEL GUIDE —

DIANA L. MITCHELL

© **Copyright 2024 - All rights reserved.**

The content contained within this book may not be reproduced, duplicated or transmitted without direct written permission from the author or the publisher.

Under no circumstances will any blame or legal responsibility be held against the publisher, or author, for any damages, reparation, or monetary loss due to the information contained within this book, either directly or indirectly.

Legal Notice:

This book is copyright protected. It is only for personal use. You cannot amend, distribute, sell, use, quote or paraphrase any part, or the content within this book, without the consent of the author or publisher.

Disclaimer Notice:

Please note the information contained within this document is for educational and entertainment purposes only. All effort has been executed to present accurate, up to date, reliable, complete information. No warranties of any kind are declared or implied. Readers acknowledge that the author is not engaged in the rendering of legal, financial, medical or professional advice. The content within this book has been derived from various sources. Please consult a licensed professional before attempting any techniques outlined in this book.

By reading this document, the reader agrees that under no circumstances is the author responsible for any losses, direct or indirect, that are incurred as a result of the use of the information contained within this document, including, but not limited to, errors, omissions, or inaccuracies.

Cover image: © MasterLu / Getty Images Pro sourced through canva.com

Dear reader, thanks a lot for purchasing my book.

To help you plan your trip even more efficiently, I have included an interactive map powered by Google My Maps.

To access it, scan the QR code below.

Happy travelling!

A Note to Our Valued Readers

Thank you for choosing this travel guide as your companion for exploring the world.

I want to take a moment to address a concern you might have regarding the absence of photographs in this book.

As an independent author and publisher, I strive to deliver high-quality, informative content at an affordable price.

Including photographs in a printed book, however, presents significant challenges. Licensing high-quality images can be extremely costly, and unfortunately, I have no control over the print quality of images within the book.

Because these guides are printed and shipped by Amazon, I am unable to review the final print quality before they reach your hands.

So, rather than risk compromising your reading experience with subpar visuals, I've chosen to focus on providing detailed, insightful content that will help you make the most of your travels.

While this guide may not contain photos, it's packed with valuable information, insider tips, and recommendations to ensure you have an enriching and memorable journey.

Additionally, there's an interactive map powered by Google My Maps—an essential tool to help you plan your trip.

I encourage you to supplement your reading with online resources where you can find up-to-date images and visuals of the destinations covered in this guide.

I hope you find this book a helpful and inspiring resource as you embark on your next adventure.

Thank you for your understanding and support.

Safe travels,

Diana

Table of Contents

- Welcome to San Francisco 1
  - Iconic Landmarks 1
  - Cultural Diversity 2
  - World-Class Museums and Art 2
  - Theater and Entertainment 2
  - Culinary Delights 2
  - Shopping Paradise 3
  - Green Spaces and Recreation 3
  - Historical Significance 3
  - Vibrant Neighborhoods 3
  - Year-Round Attractions 3
- Getting Around 5
  - Public Transportation 5
    - Muni System 5
    - BART (Bay Area Rapid Transit) 6
    - Ferry Services 7
  - Taxis and Rideshares 8
    - Yellow Cabs 8
    - Uber and Lyft 9
  - Biking 11
    - Bay Wheels Bike Share Program 11
- What to See and Do 13
  - Iconic Landmarks 13
    - Golden Gate Bridge 13
    - Alcatraz Island 14
    - Fisherman's Wharf 15
    - Pier 39 16
    - Lombard Street 17
    - Coit Tower 18
    - Palace of Fine Arts 19
    - Transamerica Pyramid 20

Painted Ladies 21
Ghirardelli Square 22
Ferry Building Marketplace 23
Twin Peaks 25
Sutro Baths 26
San Francisco City Hall 27
Grace Cathedral 28
Chinatown Gate 29
Fort Point National Historic Site 30

Museums and Cultural Institutions 33
San Francisco Museum of Modern Art (SFMOMA) 33
California Academy of Sciences 34
de Young Museum 35
Exploratorium 36
Asian Art Museum 37
Contemporary Jewish Museum 39
The Walt Disney Family Museum 40
Museum of the African Diaspora 41
Legion of Honor 42
San Francisco Cable Car Museum 44
Cartoon Art Museum 45
Beat Museum 46
Mexican Museum 47
Randall Museum 48

Theaters and Performances 51
War Memorial Opera House 51
Orpheum Theatre 52
Curran Theatre 53
American Conservatory Theater (A.C.T.) 54
Golden Gate Theatre 55
San Francisco Symphony 56
SFJAZZ Center 57

    The Fillmore 59
    Great American Music Hall 60
Historic Sites 63
    Mission San Francisco de Asís (Mission Dolores) 63
    Fort Mason 64
    Maritime National Historical Park 65
    Presidio of San Francisco 66
    Angel Island 68
    Fort Funston 69
    Balclutha Ship 70
    Haas-Lilienthal House 71
Observation Decks and Scenic Views 73
    Golden Gate Bridge Vista Point 73
    Coit Tower Observation Deck 74
    Twin Peaks Overlook 75
    de Young Museum Observation Tower 76
    The View Lounge at Marriott Marquis 77
Neighborhood Exploration 79
    North Beach 79
    Haight-Ashbury 80
    The Mission District 81
    Nob Hill 82
    Japantown 83
    Castro District 84
    Marina District 85
Food and Dining 87
    Iconic San Francisco Foods 87
        Sourdough Bread 87
        Dungeness Crab 88
        Mission-Style Burritos 88
    Fine Dining 89
        Michelin-Starred Restaurants 89

- Internationally Inspired Fine Dining 90
- Casual Eateries 90
  - Trendy Cafes and Diners 91
- Street Food and Food Trucks 92
  - Classic Street Food 92
  - Gourmet Food Trucks 92
  - Pop-Up Markets 93
- Ethnic Cuisine 93
  - North Beach 94
  - Chinatown 94
  - Mission District 95
- Food Markets 96
  - Ferry Building Marketplace 96
  - Off the Grid 96

Welcome to San Francisco

Welcome to San Francisco, a vibrant and eclectic metropolis known as the "City by the Bay." Overflowing with charm and character, San Francisco is a melting pot of cultures, flavors, and experiences, making it one of the most dynamic cities in the world. Whether you're a first-time visitor or a seasoned traveler, the city's iconic landmarks, diverse neighborhoods, and rich history offer endless opportunities for discovery and adventure.

San Francisco is composed of a variety of distinct neighborhoods, each with its own unique vibe and allure. From the lively streets of the Financial District to the bohemian spirit of Haight-Ashbury, the cultural mosaic of the Mission District, the stunning vistas of Pacific Heights, and the tranquil beauty of the Presidio, there's something for everyone in this city.

The city is home to some of the world's most iconic landmarks, such as the Golden Gate Bridge, Alcatraz Island, and Fisherman's Wharf. It's a global hub for arts, culture, and entertainment, offering world-class museums, theaters, and music venues. Whether you're exploring the lush expanse of Golden Gate Park, riding a historic cable car, delving into trendy neighborhoods, or savoring diverse culinary delights, San Francisco promises an unforgettable experience.

Join us as we uncover the best of what San Francisco has to offer, providing insights and tips to help you make the most of your visit to this extraordinary city.

Iconic Landmarks

San Francisco is home to some of the world's most recognizable landmarks. From the awe-inspiring Golden Gate Bridge, a symbol of architectural excellence, to the mysterious Alcatraz Island and the bustling charm of Fisherman's Wharf, these iconic sites are essential stops for any visitor.

Cultural Diversity

San Francisco is a vibrant tapestry of cultures, with a rich mix of ethnicities and traditions. This diversity is reflected in the city's neighborhoods, festivals, and culinary offerings, providing a global experience without leaving the city.

World-Class Museums and Art

Art lovers will find a haven in San Francisco, with its exceptional museums and galleries. The San Francisco Museum of Modern Art (SFMOMA), the de Young Museum, and the Asian Art Museum feature stunning collections from around the world, while numerous smaller galleries and cultural institutions offer unique insights into various art forms and historical periods.

Theater and Entertainment

San Francisco's performing arts scene is a magnet for theater enthusiasts. From acclaimed Broadway shows to innovative local productions, there's always something new and captivating to see. Beyond the theater, the city's comedy clubs, live music venues, and eclectic performance spaces offer endless entertainment options.

Culinary Delights

San Francisco's culinary landscape is legendary, with an array of dining experiences from Michelin-starred restaurants to beloved local spots. Enjoy fresh seafood at Fisherman's Wharf, explore diverse cuisines in Chinatown and the Mission District, or indulge in artisanal treats at the Ferry Building Marketplace.

Shopping Paradise

San Francisco is a shopper's delight, featuring high-end boutiques in Union Square, trendy shops in Hayes Valley, and unique treasures in local markets. Whether you're seeking luxury fashion, vintage finds, or quirky souvenirs, the city has something for every shopper.

Green Spaces and Recreation

Amidst the urban excitement, San Francisco offers beautiful parks and green spaces. Golden Gate Park provides a tranquil escape with its gardens, lakes, and trails, while smaller parks like Dolores Park and the Presidio offer unique urban retreats.

Historical Significance

San Francisco's rich history is reflected in its numerous historical sites. Visit the Presidio and the San Francisco Maritime National Historical Park to explore the city's past and its impact on modern America.

Vibrant Neighborhoods

Each neighborhood in San Francisco has its own unique character and charm. From the artistic flair of the Mission District and the upscale elegance of Nob Hill to the eclectic spirit of the Haight and the historic ambiance of North Beach, there's always a new area to explore.

Year-Round Attractions

San Francisco offers a variety of activities and events throughout the year. Enjoy summer street festivals, fall wine country tours, winter ice skating at Union Square, and springtime blooms in Golden Gate Park.

San Francisco's dynamic energy, cultural richness, and endless opportunities make it an unforgettable destination for travelers from around the world. Whether you're visiting for a weekend or an extended stay, San Francisco promises experiences that will leave you eager to return.

Getting Around

Public Transportation

San Francisco boasts an extensive and efficient public transportation system, making it easy to navigate the city without a car. Here's an overview of the key public transportation options, including the Muni system, BART, and ferries.

Muni System

Overview:

- The San Francisco Municipal Transportation Agency (SFMTA), known as Muni, operates the city's buses, light rail, streetcars, and cable cars, providing a comprehensive network of routes across San Francisco.
- Muni runs from early morning until late at night, with some lines operating 24/7, offering a convenient and reliable mode of transportation for residents and visitors.

Muni Lines:

- The Muni system consists of various lines, including buses, light rail (Metro), historic streetcars, and iconic cable cars.
- Light rail lines are identified by letters (e.g., J, K, L, M, N, T) and run both underground and at street level.
- Bus lines are numbered and serve neighborhoods throughout the city.

Using Muni:

- Clipper Card: The standard fare payment method. Purchase and reload at vending machines, retail locations, or online. Pay-per-ride and monthly passes are available.
- MuniMobile: A mobile app for purchasing and using digital tickets.
- Maps and Apps: Muni maps are available at stations and online. Apps like NextBus and Citymapper provide real-time updates and route planning.
- Safety Tips: Stay aware of your surroundings, avoid empty cars, and keep belongings secure.

Key Stations:

- Embarcadero: Major transfer point for multiple Muni Metro lines and BART.
- Montgomery Street: Connects to BART and serves the Financial District.
- Civic Center: Key transfer station for Muni Metro and BART.
- Powell Street: Access to cable cars and BART, serving Union Square.

BART (Bay Area Rapid Transit)

Overview:

- BART is a regional transit system connecting San Francisco with the East Bay, Peninsula, and South Bay.
- Provides rapid transit service with stops in key locations, including downtown San Francisco, Oakland, Berkeley, and SFO.

Using BART:

- Clipper Card: Use the same Clipper Card as for Muni for seamless travel between systems.
- Ticket Machines: Purchase BART tickets or Clipper Card credits at station vending machines.

- Maps and Apps: BART maps are available in stations and online. Apps like BART App and Transit provide real-time updates and trip planning.

Key Stations:

- Embarcadero: Connects to multiple Muni Metro lines and serves the Financial District.
- Montgomery Street: Located in the heart of the Financial District.
- Powell Street: Serves Union Square and provides access to cable cars.
- Civic Center: Located near the Civic Center and City Hall.

Ferry Services

Overview:

- San Francisco Bay Ferry and Golden Gate Ferry provide scenic and efficient ferry services across the San Francisco Bay, connecting the city with locations such as Sausalito, Tiburon, Oakland, and Alameda.

Routes and Schedules:

- San Francisco Bay Ferry: Connects San Francisco with Oakland, Alameda, and Vallejo. Check schedules online for departure times.
- Golden Gate Ferry: Connects San Francisco with Sausalito, Tiburon, and Larkspur. Schedules are available online.

Experience:

- Scenic Views: Enjoy stunning views of the San Francisco skyline, Alcatraz, and the Golden Gate Bridge.
- Amenities: Ferries offer various amenities, including seating areas, restrooms, and sometimes food and beverage options.
- Accessibility: Ferries and terminals are fully accessible for passengers with disabilities.

Connecting Transportation:

- Ferry Building: Major terminal with access to multiple Muni lines, BART, and nearby bus stops.
- Pier 41: Located near Fisherman's Wharf with connections to Muni buses and streetcars.

San Francisco's public transportation system is extensive and user-friendly, making it easy to get around the city efficiently. Whether you're taking Muni, riding BART, or enjoying a scenic ferry ride across the Bay, you'll find a range of options to suit your travel needs.

Taxis and Rideshares

San Francisco offers a variety of taxi and rideshare options that provide convenient and flexible transportation throughout the city. Here's a detailed look at yellow cabs, Uber, and Lyft, including how to use them, fare information, and tips for a smooth ride.

Yellow Cabs

Overview:
- The iconic yellow cabs are a familiar sight in San Francisco and are regulated by the San Francisco Municipal Transportation Agency (SFMTA).
- They can be hailed on the street, found at taxi stands, or booked through apps and phone dispatch services.

How to Hail a Yellow Cab:
- Street Hailing: Stand on the curb and raise your arm when you see an available cab. An available cab's roof light will be illuminated.
- Taxi Stands: Often located near major hotels, transportation hubs, and popular attractions.
- App and Phone Dispatch: Companies like Flywheel offer app-based booking similar to rideshare services, and traditional phone dispatch is also available.

Fare Information:
- Base Fare: Starts at $3.50, with additional charges based on distance and time.
- Surcharges: Airport surcharge of $2, plus any applicable tolls for bridge crossings.
- Tolls: Any bridge or tunnel tolls are added to the fare.
- Tips: A customary tip for taxi drivers is 15-20% of the total fare.
- Payment: Accepted in cash and credit/debit cards. All cabs are equipped with card readers.

Tips for a Smooth Ride:
- Provide Clear Directions: Have your destination address ready and communicate it clearly to the driver.
- Safety: Make sure the taxi's medallion number and driver's information are displayed on the dashboard.
- Receipt: Always ask for a receipt at the end of your ride for record-keeping or in case you need to retrieve lost items.

Uber and Lyft

Overview:
- Uber and Lyft are popular rideshare services in San Francisco, offering convenient, app-based transportation options.
- These services provide a range of vehicle types, from budget-friendly rides to luxury options.

Using Uber and Lyft:
- Download the App: Available on both iOS and Android platforms.
- Create an Account: Sign up with your email, phone number, and payment information.
- Request a Ride: Enter your destination and choose the type of ride (e.g., UberX, UberPOOL, Lyft, Lyft XL).
- Track Your Ride: The app provides real-time tracking of your driver's location and estimated arrival time.
- Payment: Automatically charged to your registered payment method. Tips can be added through the app.

Fare Information:
- Base Fare: Varies by service type and time of day.

- Surge Pricing: During peak times or high demand, prices may increase due to surge pricing.
- Tolls: Any applicable bridge or tunnel tolls are added to the fare.
- Tips: Tipping is optional but appreciated and can be done through the app.

Service Options:
- UberX/Lyft: Standard ride for up to four passengers.
- UberPOOL/Lyft Shared: Shared rides with other passengers heading in the same direction, offering a lower fare.
- UberXL/Lyft XL: Larger vehicles for groups up to six passengers.
- Uber Black/Lyft Lux: Premium black car service for a more luxurious ride experience.

Tips for a Smooth Ride:
- Confirm Your Ride: Verify the driver's name, vehicle make, model, and license plate before getting in.
- Safety Features: Both apps offer safety features such as sharing your trip status with friends and family and in-app emergency assistance.
- Pickup Locations: Choose a safe and convenient pickup location, especially in busy areas.
- Ratings: Rate your driver after the ride to provide feedback on your experience.

Comparisons and Considerations
- Availability: Yellow cabs are typically more abundant in high-traffic areas like downtown and tourist hotspots, while rideshare services can be more convenient in residential neighborhoods or less busy areas.
- Cost: Rideshare fares can be more variable due to surge pricing, whereas yellow cab fares are more consistent but may include surcharges for peak times or airport pickups.
- Convenience: Rideshare apps offer the convenience of cashless payment and real-time tracking, while yellow cabs can be easily hailed on the street without the need for an app.

Whether you choose the traditional yellow cab or a modern rideshare service like Uber or Lyft, San Francisco provides a range of options to suit your transportation needs. Understanding how to use these services effectively can help you navigate the city with ease and make the most of your time in San Francisco.

Biking

Bay Wheels Bike Share Program

Overview:
- Bay Wheels is San Francisco's bike-sharing system, offering a convenient and eco-friendly way to get around the city.
- Launched in 2013, it has grown to include thousands of bikes and numerous stations across San Francisco, Oakland, Berkeley, Emeryville, and San Jose.

How Bay Wheels Works:
- Membership Options: Choose from various membership plans, including Single Ride, Day Pass, and Annual Membership.
    - Single Ride: Best for occasional users, allows a 30-minute ride for a fixed fee.
    - Day Pass: Ideal for tourists, offers unlimited 30-minute rides in a 24-hour period.
    - Annual Membership: Best for residents, includes unlimited 45-minute rides for a year.
- Finding a Bike: Use the Bay Wheels app or website to locate nearby stations and check bike availability.
- Unlocking a Bike: Use the app, your Bay Wheels key (for annual members), or a ride code to unlock a bike at any station.
- Riding and Returning: Enjoy your ride and return the bike to any Bay Wheels station. Make sure the bike is securely docked to end your ride.

Benefits of Using Bay Wheels:
- Flexibility: Easily navigate through traffic and access areas not well-served by public transportation.
- Health and Fitness: Enjoy a workout while commuting or sightseeing.
- Environmentally Friendly: Reduce your carbon footprint by opting for a bike over a car or taxi.

Tips for a Smooth Ride:
- Plan Your Route: Use the Bay Wheels app to plan safe and efficient routes.

- Follow Traffic Rules: Obey all traffic signals and signs, use bike lanes where available, and signal your turns.
- Safety Gear: Always wear a helmet and consider using reflective clothing or lights, especially at night.
- Station Availability: Check the app for docking station availability near your destination to avoid last-minute hassles.

Popular Routes and Destinations:
- Golden Gate Park: Enjoy a scenic ride through the park's bike-friendly paths.
- Embarcadero: Ride along the waterfront with stunning views of the Bay Bridge and the bay.
- Marina Green to Fort Point: Experience the beauty of the waterfront and get close to the Golden Gate Bridge.
- Mission District: Explore this vibrant neighborhood with its murals, cafes, and unique shops.

San Francisco's Bay Wheels bike-sharing program provides an accessible and enjoyable way to explore the city. Whether you're commuting to work, sightseeing, or simply enjoying a leisurely ride, Bay Wheels offers a flexible and sustainable transportation option.

What to See and Do

Iconic Landmarks

Golden Gate Bridge

The Golden Gate Bridge is arguably one of the most recognizable symbols of San Francisco and an engineering marvel that has captivated visitors since its completion in 1937. Spanning 1.7 miles across the Golden Gate Strait, this iconic suspension bridge connects San Francisco to Marin County and has been designated as one of the Wonders of the Modern World by the American Society of Civil Engineers.

The bridge's distinctive International Orange color was chosen to enhance its visibility in the fog that frequently envelops the bay. Its Art Deco design elements and sweeping main cables add to its aesthetic appeal, making it a popular subject for photographers and artists. Visitors can experience the bridge in various ways, including walking or biking across its pedestrian pathways, which offer breathtaking views of the San Francisco skyline, Alcatraz Island, and the Pacific Ocean.

The Golden Gate Bridge's construction was an impressive feat, involving innovative techniques to overcome the challenging conditions of the Golden Gate Strait. The project faced numerous obstacles, including strong tides, deep water, and frequent fog, but its successful completion marked a significant achievement in civil engineering.

At the south end of the bridge, the Golden Gate Bridge Welcome Center provides historical exhibits and information about the bridge's construction and significance. The center also has a gift shop where visitors can purchase memorabilia. For a more immersive experience, guided tours are available, offering detailed insights into the bridge's history and the story behind its creation.

The Golden Gate Bridge is not only a critical transportation link but also a symbol of San Francisco's resilience and innovation. It has inspired countless stories, artworks, and films, embedding itself in the cultural fabric of the city. Whether shrouded in fog or gleaming in the sunlight, the bridge continues to be a testament to human ingenuity and a must-see attraction for anyone visiting San Francisco.

Alcatraz Island

Alcatraz Island, often referred to simply as "The Rock," is one of San Francisco's most intriguing historical landmarks. Located 1.25 miles offshore in San Francisco Bay, the island is famous for its former federal penitentiary, which operated from 1934 to 1963. The prison housed some of America's most notorious criminals, including Al Capone, George "Machine Gun" Kelly, and Robert Stroud, the "Birdman of Alcatraz."

Originally, Alcatraz was a military fortification and later a military prison before becoming a federal penitentiary. The island's isolated location and treacherous waters made it an ideal site for a maximum-security prison, believed to be inescapable. Despite this, there were several daring escape attempts, the most famous being the 1962 escape by Frank Morris and brothers John and Clarence Anglin, which remains unsolved.

Today, Alcatraz Island is part of the Golden Gate National Recreation Area and is managed by the National Park Service. It attracts over a million visitors annually, who come to explore its rich history and natural beauty. The island offers a range of tours, including the popular audio tour, "Doing Time: The Alcatraz Cellhouse Tour," which provides a vivid narration by former inmates and guards, bringing the island's history to life.

Visitors to Alcatraz can explore the cellhouse, mess hall, library, and other parts of the prison complex. The island also features historical exhibits and displays about the Native American occupation of Alcatraz from 1969 to 1971, which was a significant event in the history of the American Indian Movement.

Beyond its historical significance, Alcatraz Island is home to diverse wildlife, including seabirds, and offers stunning views of the San Francisco skyline and the Golden Gate Bridge. The island's gardens, once tended by prison staff and inmates, have been restored and provide a peaceful contrast to the stark prison buildings.

Alcatraz Island's combination of historical intrigue, natural beauty, and cultural significance makes it a must-visit destination for anyone interested in the multifaceted history of San Francisco and the United States.

Fisherman's Wharf

Fisherman's Wharf is one of San Francisco's most popular and vibrant neighborhoods, known for its rich maritime history, bustling piers, and lively atmosphere. Located on the northern waterfront, this iconic area offers a unique blend of historical charm, entertainment, and culinary delights, making it a must-visit destination for tourists and locals alike.

Historically, Fisherman's Wharf has been the center of San Francisco's fishing industry since the mid-1800s. The area was originally settled by Italian immigrant fishermen who introduced the city's now-famous Dungeness crab. Today, visitors can still see fishing boats at work and buy fresh seafood directly from the docks, maintaining the neighborhood's authentic maritime character.

One of the main attractions at Fisherman's Wharf is Pier 39, a bustling commercial area that features a wide variety of shops, restaurants, and family-friendly attractions. Here, visitors can enjoy watching the playful sea lions that have made the pier their home, ride the carousel, or take in the views of Alcatraz Island and the Golden Gate Bridge. Pier 39 is also home to the Aquarium of the Bay, which offers an immersive experience of the marine life found in San Francisco Bay.

Ghirardelli Square, another highlight of Fisherman's Wharf, is a historic chocolate factory turned shopping and dining complex. Visitors can indulge in world-famous Ghirardelli chocolate, enjoy a meal at one of the many restaurants, or browse the unique boutiques housed within the beautifully restored brick buildings.

Fisherman's Wharf is also known for its diverse dining options, particularly its seafood. From casual food stalls offering clam chowder in sourdough bread bowls to upscale restaurants with stunning waterfront views, there is something to satisfy every palate. Popular spots include Boudin Bakery, known for its sourdough bread, and Alioto's, a family-run restaurant that has been serving fresh seafood since 1925.

In addition to its culinary offerings, Fisherman's Wharf hosts several museums and historical sites. The San Francisco Maritime National Historical Park includes a fleet of historic ships, a visitor center, and the Maritime Museum, which provides insight into the city's seafaring past. The nearby Musée Mécanique is an interactive museum featuring a vast collection of antique arcade machines and mechanical musical instruments.

Fisherman's Wharf's lively atmosphere, rich history, and diverse attractions make it an essential stop for anyone visiting San Francisco. Whether you're exploring the waterfront, enjoying the fresh seafood, or soaking in the vibrant street performances, Fisherman's Wharf offers a quintessential San Francisco experience.

Pier 39

Pier 39 is one of San Francisco's premier attractions, offering visitors a unique blend of entertainment, dining, shopping, and stunning views. Located on the waterfront at the edge of Fisherman's Wharf, Pier 39 has become a bustling hub of activity since its opening in 1978.

One of the most beloved features of Pier 39 is its resident sea lions. After the 1989 Loma Prieta earthquake, a group of sea lions took up residence on the pier's floating docks, and they have been a major draw ever since. Visitors can watch these playful and noisy animals up close, a delightful experience for both adults and children.

In addition to the sea lions, Pier 39 is home to the Aquarium of the Bay, which offers an immersive journey through the underwater world of San Francisco Bay. With its walk-through tunnel exhibits and touch pools, the aquarium provides a hands-on learning experience about the bay's diverse marine life.

Pier 39 also boasts a wide variety of dining options, ranging from casual food stalls to sit-down restaurants with spectacular views of the bay. The pier is famous for its seafood, particularly clam chowder served in sourdough bread bowls, a San Francisco staple. Restaurants like Fog Harbor Fish House and Pier Market Seafood Restaurant are popular choices for fresh, locally sourced seafood dishes.

Shoppers will find plenty to explore at Pier 39, with an eclectic mix of boutiques and specialty stores. From souvenirs and gifts to clothing and accessories, there is something for everyone. Notable shops include the Alcatraz Gift Shop and the NFL Shop, offering unique items that make perfect mementos of your visit.

Entertainment is a key component of the Pier 39 experience. Street performers, magicians, and musicians provide live entertainment throughout the day, adding to the lively atmosphere. The pier also features a two-story carousel, offering fun rides for children and nostalgic moments for adults.

The location of Pier 39 offers breathtaking views of some of San Francisco's most iconic landmarks, including Alcatraz Island, the Golden Gate Bridge, and the Bay Bridge. The picturesque setting makes it an ideal spot for photography enthusiasts and those simply looking to enjoy the scenery.

Overall, Pier 39 is a vibrant and multifaceted destination that captures the essence of San Francisco's waterfront culture. Whether you're dining, shopping, or simply enjoying the views and sea lions, Pier 39 promises an unforgettable experience for visitors of all ages.

Lombard Street

Lombard Street is one of San Francisco's most famous and visually striking landmarks, renowned for its unique and winding design. Located between Hyde and Leavenworth Streets in the Russian Hill neighborhood, Lombard Street is often referred to as the "Crookedest Street in the World," though it is technically not the most crooked street in San Francisco—a title held by Vermont Street.

The block of Lombard Street between Hyde and Leavenworth features eight sharp hairpin turns, which were designed to reduce the street's natural steep gradient of 27%. This distinctive design was introduced in the 1920s to improve safety for vehicles descending the steep slope. Today, the brick-paved road is lined with beautifully landscaped gardens, vibrant flowerbeds, and charming residential houses, making it a picturesque and popular tourist destination.

Visitors to Lombard Street can experience its unique charm in several ways. Driving down the winding section is a popular activity, though it requires careful navigation due to the tight turns and frequent pedestrian traffic. For those who prefer a more leisurely pace, walking along the sidewalks that flank the road provides an opportunity to take in the street's beauty and snap photographs of the iconic curves.

At the top of Lombard Street, visitors are treated to stunning views of the San Francisco Bay, Alcatraz Island, and Coit Tower. The vista is particularly impressive on clear days, offering a panoramic perspective of the city's skyline and waterfront. The Hyde Street cable car line runs directly past the top of Lombard Street, making it easily accessible for tourists.

The street's charming aesthetics and historical significance have made it a frequent feature in films, television shows, and postcards, cementing its status as a symbol of San Francisco. While it may be a short stretch of road, Lombard Street's winding design and lush surroundings create a unique and memorable experience for all who visit.

Lombard Street's blend of architectural ingenuity, natural beauty, and historical charm makes it a must-see destination for anyone exploring San Francisco. Whether you're driving, walking, or simply admiring the view, Lombard Street offers a quintessential San Francisco experience that captures the city's distinctive character and allure.

Coit Tower

Perched atop Telegraph Hill, Coit Tower is one of San Francisco's most recognizable landmarks, offering panoramic views of the city and the bay. The 210-foot tower, constructed in 1933, is an enduring symbol of San Francisco's skyline and a testament to the city's rich history and cultural heritage.

Coit Tower was funded by Lillie Hitchcock Coit, a wealthy socialite and philanthropist with a passion for firefighting. In her will, she left a substantial sum of money "for the purpose of adding to the beauty of the city I have always loved." The resulting tower, designed by architects Arthur Brown, Jr. and Henry Howard, was built in the Art Deco style and stands as a tribute to San Francisco's firefighters.

One of the most compelling features of Coit Tower is its collection of murals, which adorn the interior walls. These murals were painted in 1934 as part of the Public Works of Art Project, a New Deal program designed to provide employment for artists during the Great Depression. The murals, created by 27 different artists, depict various aspects of life in California during the 1930s, from agriculture and industry to education and recreation. The murals are notable for their social realism style and provide a fascinating glimpse into the era's daily life and struggles.

Visitors to Coit Tower can take an elevator to the top for a small fee, where they are rewarded with sweeping views of San Francisco. From the observation deck, one can see landmarks such as the Golden Gate Bridge, Alcatraz Island, the Bay Bridge, and the downtown skyline. The tower's hilltop location makes it an ideal vantage point for photography and sightseeing, especially on clear days when visibility is at its best.

The surrounding area, known as Pioneer Park, offers a serene setting for a leisurely stroll. The park's lush greenery and well-maintained paths provide a pleasant escape from the bustling city below. The hike up Telegraph Hill can be a bit steep, but the effort is well worth it for the views and the chance to explore one of San Francisco's most iconic sites.

Coit Tower's historical significance, stunning murals, and breathtaking views make it a must-visit destination for anyone traveling to San Francisco. Whether you're an art enthusiast, a history buff, or simply someone who appreciates beautiful vistas, Coit Tower offers something for everyone and remains a beloved symbol of the city's enduring spirit and charm.

Palace of Fine Arts

The Palace of Fine Arts is one of San Francisco's most enchanting landmarks, renowned for its stunning classical architecture and tranquil setting. Located in the Marina District, this monumental structure was originally constructed for the 1915 Panama-Pacific International Exposition, an event celebrating the completion of the Panama Canal and San Francisco's recovery from the 1906 earthquake.

Designed by architect Bernard Maybeck, the Palace of Fine Arts is a masterpiece of Beaux-Arts architecture, inspired by Roman and Greek structures. The central rotunda, with its magnificent dome and Corinthian columns, is surrounded by a serene lagoon and beautifully landscaped gardens. The intricate sculptures and reliefs adorning the structure add to its timeless elegance, making it a popular spot for photographers and artists.

The Palace of Fine Arts was initially intended to house art exhibitions during the exposition, but its popularity and beauty ensured its preservation long after the event ended. Over the years, it has undergone several restorations to maintain its grandeur, with the most significant renovation completed in 1964. Today, the palace serves as a cultural hub, hosting various events, exhibitions, and performances.

One of the most appealing aspects of the Palace of Fine Arts is its picturesque setting. The lagoon, home to swans and ducks, reflects the majestic structure, creating a serene and idyllic atmosphere. Visitors can enjoy a leisurely stroll around the grounds, take in the views from the park benches, or have a picnic on the lush lawns.

The Palace of Fine Arts Theater, located within the complex, is an intimate venue that hosts a variety of performances, including concerts, plays, and lectures. The theater's impressive acoustics and elegant design make it a favorite among performers and audiences alike.

The Palace of Fine Arts is not only a testament to San Francisco's artistic heritage but also a symbol of the city's resilience and cultural vibrancy. Its timeless beauty and serene ambiance make it a must-visit destination for anyone exploring San Francisco, offering a perfect blend of history, art, and natural beauty.

Transamerica Pyramid

The Transamerica Pyramid is an iconic symbol of San Francisco's skyline, renowned for its distinctive triangular shape and modern architectural design. Located in the Financial District, this skyscraper stands at 853 feet, making it the second-tallest building in San Francisco and a prominent feature of the city's urban landscape.

Designed by architect William Pereira and completed in 1972, the Transamerica Pyramid was originally conceived as the headquarters for the Transamerica Corporation. Its unique design was intended to maximize natural light and ventilation while minimizing wind resistance. The building's four-sided pyramid shape, with its sharp angles and tapered form, sets it apart from traditional rectangular skyscrapers, giving it a futuristic and dynamic appearance.

One of the most striking features of the Transamerica Pyramid is its spire, which extends 212 feet above the top floor, bringing the total height to 853 feet. The spire is illuminated at night, creating a beacon that can be seen from various points around the city. The building's exterior is clad in white quartz, which glows in the sunlight and gives the structure a clean, sleek look.

Although the Transamerica Pyramid is not open to the public for tours, visitors can still appreciate its architectural beauty from the surrounding area. The Redwood Park at the base of the pyramid offers a peaceful retreat with its towering redwood trees, water features, and sculptures. The park provides a perfect vantage point for viewing the skyscraper and enjoying a moment of tranquility in the heart of the bustling Financial District.

The Transamerica Pyramid is more than just a striking piece of architecture; it is a symbol of San Francisco's innovation and forward-thinking spirit. Its distinctive silhouette has become an integral part of the city's identity, often featured in films, television shows, and postcards.

For those interested in learning more about the building's history and design, the Transamerica Pyramid Center offers an informative visitor experience with displays and exhibits detailing the skyscraper's construction and significance. Whether admired from afar or explored up close, the Transamerica Pyramid remains a testament to San Francisco's architectural prowess and creative vision.

Painted Ladies

The Painted Ladies are a row of picturesque Victorian houses, renowned for their colorful facades and ornate detailing. Located on Steiner Street, across from Alamo Square Park, these historic homes are one of San Francisco's most photographed landmarks and a quintessential example of the city's architectural heritage.

Constructed during the late 19th century, the Painted Ladies exemplify the Victorian and Edwardian styles that were prevalent in San Francisco before the 1906 earthquake. These houses are characterized by their steep gable roofs, turrets, bay windows, and intricate woodwork. The term "Painted Ladies" was coined in the 1970s to describe Victorian houses that have been painted in three or more colors to enhance their architectural details.

The most famous cluster of Painted Ladies is known as "Postcard Row," located at 710-720 Steiner Street. This row of seven houses gained widespread recognition when they were featured in the opening credits of the television show "Full House." Their vibrant colors and picturesque setting against the backdrop of downtown San Francisco create a stunning visual contrast that attracts visitors from around the world.

Alamo Square Park, directly across from the Painted Ladies, offers one of the best vantage points for viewing and photographing these iconic homes. The park's elevated location provides sweeping views of the city skyline, making it a popular spot for picnics, leisurely strolls, and photo opportunities. The lush lawns, blooming flower beds, and historic lamp posts add to the park's charm and provide a serene environment to admire the architectural beauty of the Painted Ladies.

The Painted Ladies are not just aesthetically pleasing; they also represent the resilience and history of San Francisco. Many of these homes survived the 1906 earthquake and subsequent fires, and their preservation is a testament to the city's commitment to maintaining its architectural heritage. Over the years, the Painted Ladies have been meticulously restored and maintained by their owners, ensuring that they continue to be a vibrant part of the city's landscape.

Visiting the Painted Ladies offers a glimpse into San Francisco's rich architectural history and a chance to appreciate the craftsmanship and artistry of the Victorian era. Whether you're an architecture enthusiast or simply looking to capture a quintessential San Francisco scene, the Painted Ladies are a must-see destination that encapsulates the charm and elegance of the city.

Ghirardelli Square

Ghirardelli Square is a historic and vibrant landmark located in the Fisherman's Wharf area of San Francisco. Originally the site of the Ghirardelli Chocolate Company, it has been transformed into a bustling shopping, dining, and entertainment complex while retaining much of its historic charm. The square, named after Italian chocolatier Domenico Ghirardelli, is a testament to the city's rich history and entrepreneurial spirit.

Founded in 1852, the Ghirardelli Chocolate Company quickly became a San Francisco institution, known for its high-quality chocolate products. The factory operated at this location from 1893 until the early 1960s, when it was repurposed into a public square. The renovation preserved the original brick buildings and iconic Ghirardelli sign, blending historical architecture with modern amenities.

Today, Ghirardelli Square is a popular destination for both locals and tourists. The centerpiece is the Ghirardelli Chocolate Shop and Soda Fountain, where visitors can indulge in an array of decadent treats, including the famous hot fudge sundae and world-renowned chocolate squares. Watching the chocolate-making process through the large windows adds to the delightful experience.

Beyond chocolate, Ghirardelli Square offers a variety of shopping and dining options. Unique boutiques and specialty stores provide a range of goods, from artisan crafts to high-end fashion. The diverse dining establishments cater to all tastes, featuring everything from casual eateries to upscale restaurants. McCormick & Kuleto's, known for its fresh seafood and stunning views of the bay, is a notable dining option.

The square's picturesque setting and historic ambiance make it a perfect spot for leisurely strolls and photo opportunities. The outdoor plaza is often animated with live music, festivals, and seasonal events, creating a lively and inviting atmosphere. The views of San Francisco Bay, Alcatraz Island, and the Golden Gate Bridge add to the square's allure, offering a scenic backdrop for any visit.

Ghirardelli Square is more than just a shopping and dining destination; it is a cultural landmark that celebrates San Francisco's heritage and the legacy of one of its pioneering businesses. Whether you're savoring a chocolate treat, exploring the shops, or enjoying the views, Ghirardelli Square provides a quintessential San Francisco experience that blends history, flavor, and charm.

Ferry Building Marketplace

The Ferry Building Marketplace is one of San Francisco's most iconic and beloved landmarks, renowned for its vibrant food scene, rich history, and stunning waterfront location. Situated at the foot of Market Street along the Embarcadero, the Ferry Building has been a hub of activity since it opened in 1898, serving as the primary terminal for ferries traveling across San Francisco Bay.

The building's Beaux-Arts architecture, complete with its signature clock tower, stands as a testament to San Francisco's architectural heritage. Inside, the marketplace has been meticulously restored to preserve its historical charm while accommodating a bustling array of modern vendors. The result is a dynamic space that blends the old with the new, offering visitors a unique culinary and cultural experience.

The Ferry Building Marketplace is a food lover's paradise, featuring a diverse array of artisan producers, specialty food shops, and gourmet restaurants. Visitors can explore an assortment of culinary delights, from fresh oysters and artisanal cheeses to hand-crafted chocolates and locally roasted coffee. Notable vendors include Hog Island Oyster Co., known for its fresh, sustainably harvested oysters, and Cowgirl Creamery, which offers a selection of award-winning cheeses.

In addition to its permanent vendors, the Ferry Building hosts the Ferry Plaza Farmers Market, one of the best farmers markets in the country. Held three times a week (Tuesdays, Thursdays, and Saturdays), the market brings together local farmers, ranchers, and food artisans who offer the finest seasonal produce, meats, and prepared foods. The market is a favorite among locals and chefs alike, known for its high-quality offerings and vibrant atmosphere.

Beyond food, the Ferry Building Marketplace also houses unique retail shops that sell everything from kitchenware and cookbooks to handcrafted jewelry and home goods. These shops provide an opportunity to find one-of-a-kind items and gifts that reflect the creativity and craftsmanship of the Bay Area.

The Ferry Building's waterfront location offers breathtaking views of the Bay Bridge, Treasure Island, and the bustling bay itself. Visitors can enjoy a meal or a snack at one of the outdoor tables, taking in the scenic surroundings and lively atmosphere. The building's proximity to public transportation, including ferries, buses, and the historic F-Line streetcar, makes it easily accessible from all parts of the city.

Whether you're a foodie, a history buff, or simply looking to enjoy a quintessential San Francisco experience, the Ferry Building Marketplace is a must-visit destination. Its blend of culinary excellence, historical significance, and scenic beauty makes it a true gem of the city.

Twin Peaks

Twin Peaks is one of San Francisco's most iconic natural landmarks, offering panoramic views of the city and beyond. Located near the geographical center of the city, these two prominent hills, known as "North Peak" and "South Peak," rise about 922 feet above sea level, making them the second-highest points in San Francisco. The breathtaking vistas from Twin Peaks attract tourists and locals alike, making it a must-visit destination for anyone exploring the city.

The Twin Peaks provide a 360-degree view of San Francisco and the surrounding Bay Area, including the Golden Gate Bridge, Bay Bridge, downtown skyline, Alcatraz Island, and the rolling hills of Marin County. On clear days, visitors can see as far as the East Bay and the Pacific Ocean. The stunning sunsets and occasional fog rolling over the hills add a dramatic touch to the already spectacular scenery.

Access to Twin Peaks is relatively easy, with a winding road, Twin Peaks Boulevard, leading up to the summit. There is ample parking available, as well as a few designated viewpoints with informational plaques that provide insights into the history and geography of the area. For those who prefer an active approach, several hiking trails lead up to the peaks, offering a more immersive experience of the natural surroundings.

One of the most popular trails is the Twin Peaks Trail, which starts near the base of the hills and winds its way up through a mix of open grasslands and eucalyptus groves. The hike provides not only physical exercise but also opportunities to observe local wildlife and native plants. The area is home to various species of birds, including hawks and owls, making it a great spot for birdwatching.

At the summit, the Sutro Tower, a massive television and radio antenna, stands as a notable landmark. While the tower itself is not open to the public, it adds to the distinctive skyline of the Twin Peaks and is an important part of San Francisco's broadcasting infrastructure.

Twin Peaks is also a popular spot for nighttime visits. The city lights create a dazzling display that can be enjoyed from the various viewpoints, offering a different yet equally captivating perspective of San Francisco.

Whether you're visiting during the day or at night, Twin Peaks offers a unique vantage point to appreciate the beauty and diversity of San Francisco. Its combination of easy accessibility, breathtaking views, and natural beauty makes it a highlight of any trip to the city, providing unforgettable memories and countless photo opportunities.

Sutro Baths

The Sutro Baths, located at the western edge of San Francisco near the Pacific Ocean, are a fascinating historical site that offers visitors a glimpse into the city's past. Once the largest indoor swimming complex in the world, the Sutro Baths were a marvel of engineering and leisure when they opened in 1896. Today, the ruins of the baths are part of the Golden Gate National Recreation Area, attracting history enthusiasts, photographers, and nature lovers.

The baths were the brainchild of Adolph Sutro, a wealthy entrepreneur and former mayor of San Francisco. Sutro envisioned a grand public bathhouse that would provide affordable recreation for the city's residents. The complex featured seven saltwater swimming pools of varying temperatures, a freshwater pool, slides, trapezes, and springboards. It also housed a museum, an amphitheater, and a skating rink, making it a comprehensive entertainment venue.

Despite its grandeur, the Sutro Baths faced financial difficulties and changing public tastes, leading to its decline. In 1966, a fire destroyed much of the remaining structure, and the site was never rebuilt. Today, visitors can explore the ruins of the baths, which include remnants of the concrete pools, tunnels, and the foundations of the original buildings. The site's rugged beauty, combined with the crashing waves of the Pacific Ocean, creates a hauntingly beautiful landscape.

The Sutro Baths are accessible via a network of trails that wind through the Lands End area. The Lands End Trail, in particular, offers stunning views of the coastline, the Golden Gate Bridge, and the Marin Headlands. Interpretive signs along the trail provide historical context and information about the local flora and fauna.

For those interested in the history of the Sutro Baths, the nearby Cliff House Visitor Center offers exhibits and artifacts related to the site's past. The visitor center provides a deeper understanding of Adolph Sutro's vision and the baths' significance in San Francisco's history.

The Sutro Baths are not only a testament to the city's innovative spirit but also a serene spot for reflection and exploration. Whether you're drawn by the history, the scenic beauty, or the sense of adventure, the Sutro Baths offer a unique and memorable experience in San Francisco.

San Francisco City Hall

San Francisco City Hall is a magnificent example of Beaux-Arts architecture and a symbol of the city's rich history and civic pride. Located in the Civic Center area, this grand building has been the seat of government for the City and County of San Francisco since its completion in 1915. Its impressive dome, which rises 307 feet above the ground, is one of the tallest in the world and dominates the skyline of the Civic Center.

Designed by renowned architect Arthur Brown, Jr., City Hall's construction was part of a major urban renewal project following the devastation of the 1906 earthquake and fire. The building's grandiose design reflects the optimism and ambition of the era, featuring a stunning rotunda, grand staircases, and intricate marble and gold detailing.

The interior of San Francisco City Hall is equally impressive, with its vast open spaces and elegant decor. The rotunda, with its soaring dome and expansive floor, is a popular spot for weddings, events, and ceremonies. The sweeping grand staircase, often referred to as the "Grand Staircase," leads visitors up to the upper levels, where the mayor's office and various governmental chambers are located.

One of the highlights of City Hall is the Rotunda Gallery, which showcases art exhibitions and historical displays. These exhibits often focus on San Francisco's rich cultural heritage and diverse communities, providing a deeper understanding of the city's history and identity.

Visitors to City Hall can take guided tours, which offer insights into the building's architecture, history, and the workings of city government. The tours provide access to areas not typically open to the public, such as the legislative chambers and the mayor's office.

City Hall's Civic Center location places it in the heart of San Francisco's cultural and governmental district. Nearby attractions include the War Memorial Opera House, the Asian Art Museum, and the San Francisco Public Library. The expansive Civic Center Plaza, located in front of City

Hall, hosts numerous events, festivals, and public gatherings throughout the year.

San Francisco City Hall is more than just a governmental building; it is a symbol of the city's resilience, history, and commitment to civic engagement. Whether you're interested in architecture, history, or politics, a visit to City Hall offers a fascinating glimpse into the heart of San Francisco.

Grace Cathedral

Grace Cathedral is one of San Francisco's most majestic and spiritually significant landmarks, renowned for its striking Gothic Revival architecture, stunning stained glass windows, and inclusive community. Located atop Nob Hill, this Episcopal cathedral has been a center of worship, reflection, and social justice since its founding.

The current Grace Cathedral was constructed between 1928 and 1964, following the destruction of the original Grace Church in the 1906 earthquake. Designed by architect Lewis P. Hobart, the cathedral draws inspiration from French Gothic cathedrals, evident in its grand façade, twin towers, and intricately carved details. The cathedral's labyrinths, both indoor and outdoor, are based on the famous labyrinth at Chartres Cathedral in France and are open to the public for meditation and contemplation.

One of the most striking features of Grace Cathedral is its array of stained glass windows, which depict scenes from the Bible, historical events, and modern themes. These vibrant windows fill the cathedral with colorful light and create a serene and contemplative atmosphere. The rose window, located above the main entrance, is particularly notable for its intricate design and symbolism.

Inside, the cathedral houses several works of art and historical artifacts. The AIDS Interfaith Memorial Chapel, dedicated to those affected by the AIDS epidemic, features a poignant altarpiece by artist Keith Haring. The altarpiece, one of Haring's final works before his death from AIDS-related complications, serves as a powerful symbol of hope and remembrance.

Grace Cathedral is also known for its commitment to social justice and community service. The cathedral hosts a variety of programs and events, including art exhibitions, concerts, lectures, and interfaith services. Its Choir of Men and Boys, established in 1913, is one of the oldest cathedral choirs in the United States and performs regularly at services and special events.

Visitors to Grace Cathedral can explore its beautiful interior, walk the labyrinths, and attend services and events. Guided tours are available, offering insights into the cathedral's history, architecture, and mission. The cathedral's location on Nob Hill provides stunning views of the city and easy access to other historic sites and attractions.

Grace Cathedral is not only a place of worship but also a cultural and spiritual landmark that welcomes people of all backgrounds. Its architectural beauty, rich history, and commitment to inclusivity make it a must-visit destination for anyone exploring San Francisco. Whether you're seeking spiritual solace, artistic inspiration, or a deeper understanding of the city's heritage, Grace Cathedral offers a unique and enriching experience.

Chinatown Gate

The Chinatown Gate, also known as the Dragon Gate, is a symbolic entrance to San Francisco's Chinatown, the oldest Chinatown in North America and one of the largest Chinese communities outside Asia. Located at the intersection of Grant Avenue and Bush Street, this iconic landmark serves as a grand welcome to visitors entering the vibrant and culturally rich neighborhood.

The Chinatown Gate was a gift from the Republic of China (Taiwan) and was designed by Chinese-American architect Clayton Lee, completed in 1970. It features traditional Chinese architectural elements, including a pagoda-style roof adorned with green tiles and upturned eaves. Two guardian lions, known as "Fu Dogs," stand at the base of the gate, symbolizing protection and good fortune. The gate's inscription, written by calligrapher C.C. Wang, translates to "All under heaven is for the good of the people," reflecting the inclusive and communal spirit of the area.

Beyond its architectural beauty, the Chinatown Gate marks the beginning of Grant Avenue, the main thoroughfare of Chinatown. This bustling street is lined with colorful shops, restaurants, and markets offering a wide array of goods, from traditional Chinese herbs and teas to modern souvenirs and gifts. The area is a sensory delight, with the aroma of freshly cooked dim sum wafting through the air, the vibrant red and gold decorations, and the lively chatter of vendors and visitors.

Chinatown itself is a treasure trove of cultural experiences and historical significance. Visitors can explore the many attractions within walking distance of the gate, such as the Chinese Historical Society of America Museum, which offers insights into the history and contributions of Chinese Americans, and the Tin How Temple, one of the oldest Chinese temples in the United States.

The Chinatown Gate also serves as the starting point for numerous cultural festivals and parades, including the famous Chinese New Year Parade, which draws thousands of spectators each year. These events showcase traditional Chinese music, dance, and martial arts, adding to the area's vibrant cultural tapestry.

In summary, the Chinatown Gate is not just an entrance but a symbol of San Francisco's rich cultural diversity and the enduring legacy of its Chinese community. Whether you're exploring the historic streets, sampling authentic cuisine, or participating in cultural celebrations, the Chinatown Gate offers a captivating introduction to one of the city's most dynamic neighborhoods.

Fort Point National Historic Site

Fort Point National Historic Site is a remarkable historical landmark located at the southern base of the Golden Gate Bridge in San Francisco. This impressive brick fort, built between 1853 and 1861, played a critical role in the defense of San Francisco Bay during the American Civil War. Today, it stands as a testament to the city's rich military history and offers visitors a unique glimpse into the past.

Designed in the style of Third System fortifications, Fort Point was constructed by the United States Army Corps of Engineers to protect San Francisco from potential naval attacks. Its strategic location provided a clear line of sight over the Golden Gate Strait, making it an ideal spot for a coastal defense fort. The fort is notable for its casemates, large vaulted rooms designed to house cannons, which provided a formidable line of defense.

Although Fort Point never saw combat, it remains an engineering marvel of its time. The fort's four tiers of artillery emplacements, robust masonry construction, and innovative design elements showcase the advanced military architecture of the mid-19th century. The fort's construction required significant engineering prowess, given the challenging conditions of the site, including strong tides, wind, and fog.

Today, Fort Point is preserved as part of the Golden Gate National Recreation Area and is open to the public. Visitors can explore the fort's interior, including its barracks, officers' quarters, and the massive brick arches that support the structure. The top level of the fort offers stunning views of the Golden Gate Bridge, San Francisco Bay, and the Marin Headlands, making it a popular spot for photography and sightseeing.

The site also features a museum with exhibits detailing the fort's history, construction, and role in coastal defense. Rangers and volunteers provide guided tours and educational programs, offering deeper insights into the fort's significance and the daily lives of the soldiers stationed there.

Fort Point's unique location beneath the Golden Gate Bridge adds to its allure. The juxtaposition of the 19th-century fort with the modern engineering marvel of the bridge creates a striking visual contrast and highlights the evolution of military and civil engineering over the past century.

In summary, Fort Point National Historic Site is a fascinating destination that combines historical significance, architectural beauty, and breathtaking scenery. Whether you're a history buff, an architecture enthusiast, or simply looking for a scenic spot to explore, Fort Point offers a rich and rewarding experience that captures the essence of San Francisco's storicd past.

Museums and Cultural Institutions

San Francisco Museum of Modern Art (SFMOMA)

The San Francisco Museum of Modern Art (SFMOMA) is a premier destination for contemporary art enthusiasts, renowned for its expansive collection and innovative exhibitions. Located in the vibrant SoMa (South of Market) district, SFMOMA has been a cultural cornerstone since its opening in 1935. The museum underwent a significant expansion and reopened in 2016 with nearly triple its previous gallery space, making it one of the largest modern art museums in the world.

Designed by the acclaimed architecture firm Snøhetta, the expanded SFMOMA features a striking, undulating facade that contrasts with the geometric lines of the original Mario Botta building. The new design includes seven floors of gallery space, a rooftop garden, and an atrium that floods the interior with natural light, creating an inviting and dynamic environment for art appreciation.

SFMOMA's collection spans a wide range of mediums, including painting, sculpture, photography, architecture, design, and media arts. It houses over 33,000 works of art, featuring masterpieces by artists such as Jackson Pollock, Andy Warhol, Mark Rothko, and Gerhard Richter. The museum is particularly known for its impressive holdings of works by American and European modernists, as well as its commitment to showcasing emerging and underrepresented artists.

One of the highlights of SFMOMA is its Pritzker Center for Photography, the largest space in the country dedicated to photography within a modern art museum. The center hosts rotating exhibitions that explore the history and evolution of photographic art, from early daguerreotypes to contemporary digital works.

In addition to its permanent collection, SFMOMA offers a dynamic schedule of temporary exhibitions, educational programs, and public events. These include artist talks, film screenings, and interactive workshops designed to engage visitors of all ages and backgrounds.

The museum's amenities further enhance the visitor experience, with a range of dining options, including the Michelin-starred In Situ restaurant, which features a menu inspired by the art on display. The museum store offers a curated selection of art books, design objects, and unique gifts.

SFMOMA is not just a place to view art but a vibrant cultural hub that fosters creativity, dialogue, and inspiration. Whether you're a seasoned art lover or a curious newcomer, SFMOMA offers a rich and immersive experience that celebrates the transformative power of modern and contemporary art.

California Academy of Sciences

The California Academy of Sciences, located in San Francisco's Golden Gate Park, is one of the most innovative and environmentally-focused museums in the world. As a leading scientific and cultural institution, the Academy combines a natural history museum, an aquarium, a planetarium, and a rainforest all under one living roof, offering a truly unique and immersive experience for visitors.

The Academy's current building, designed by renowned architect Renzo Piano and opened in 2008, is a marvel of sustainable architecture. The structure features a 2.5-acre living roof covered with native plants, which helps insulate the building, reduce runoff, and provide habitat for local wildlife. The building itself is LEED Platinum certified, reflecting the Academy's commitment to environmental stewardship.

One of the standout attractions at the California Academy of Sciences is the Steinhart Aquarium, home to more than 38,000 live animals representing over 900 species. The aquarium features a range of habitats, from the depths of a Philippine coral reef to the flooded forests of the Amazon. Highlights include the stunning coral reef exhibit, the tranquil penguin colony, and the interactive touch pools where visitors can get hands-on with marine life.

Another major draw is the Morrison Planetarium, the largest all-digital planetarium in the world. With its state-of-the-art projection system, the planetarium offers breathtaking shows that explore the universe's wonders, from our solar system to the farthest reaches of space. These shows are both visually spectacular and scientifically informative, making them a favorite for visitors of all ages.

The Osher Rainforest, a four-story dome within the Academy, replicates the diverse ecosystems of a tropical rainforest. Visitors can walk through spiraling pathways surrounded by free-flying birds, butterflies, and over 1,600 live plants. The experience culminates in an underwater tunnel where visitors can view the rainforest from below, watching fish and other aquatic species swim overhead.

The Kimball Natural History Museum within the Academy features exhibits on a wide range of topics, including geology, evolution, and biodiversity. Notable exhibits include a towering T. rex skeleton, the Foucault pendulum, and the Altered State exhibit, which explores the effects of climate change on California's ecosystems.

The California Academy of Sciences is not just a museum but a dynamic center for scientific research and education. It offers a variety of programs, workshops, and lectures aimed at fostering a deeper understanding of the natural world. Whether you're exploring the depths of the ocean, the far reaches of space, or the vibrant life of a rainforest, the Academy provides an engaging and educational experience that inspires a sense of wonder and a commitment to conservation.

de Young Museum

The de Young Museum, located in San Francisco's Golden Gate Park, is a premier fine arts museum renowned for its diverse collection, innovative exhibitions, and striking architecture. Originally established in 1895, the museum was reimagined and reopened in 2005 with a modern design by architects Herzog & de Meuron, making it a significant cultural landmark in the city.

The museum's exterior is clad in perforated copper, which allows the building to blend harmoniously with the natural surroundings of Golden Gate Park as the metal ages and changes color. The building's distinctive design also includes a 144-foot observation tower that offers panoramic views of the park, the city, and the Golden Gate Bridge, providing a unique vantage point for visitors.

Inside, the de Young Museum boasts an extensive collection of American art from the 17th through the 21st centuries, including paintings, sculptures, decorative arts, and textiles. The museum is particularly noted for its holdings of American art from the 1800s to the present, featuring works by prominent artists such as John Singer Sargent, Grant Wood, Georgia O'Keeffe, and Richard Diebenkorn.

The de Young also houses an impressive collection of art from Africa, Oceania, and the Americas. This includes a diverse array of objects such as ceremonial masks, textiles, and sculptures that highlight the rich cultural traditions and artistic achievements of indigenous peoples. The museum's collection of ancient art from the Americas features significant artifacts from Mesoamerica, the Andes, and the Caribbean, offering insights into the artistic practices and cultural histories of these regions.

Temporary exhibitions at the de Young Museum are a major draw, often featuring blockbuster shows that attract international attention. Past exhibitions have included works by artists such as Diego Rivera, David Hockney, and Jean-Michel Basquiat, as well as thematic exhibitions exploring topics like fashion, photography, and contemporary art.

The de Young Museum is also dedicated to educational and community outreach, offering a variety of programs, workshops, and lectures designed to engage visitors of all ages. The museum's Friday Nights at the de Young series provides an opportunity for the public to enjoy live music, performances, and art-making activities in a social and dynamic setting.

The museum's amenities include a café, a museum store offering a selection of art books, jewelry, and gifts, and beautifully landscaped sculpture gardens that provide a peaceful retreat within the bustling park.

In summary, the de Young Museum is a cultural treasure that offers a rich and varied experience for art lovers and visitors interested in exploring the intersections of art, culture, and history. Its compelling exhibitions, extensive collections, and innovative architecture make it a must-visit destination in San Francisco.

Exploratorium

The Exploratorium, located at Pier 15 on San Francisco's Embarcadero, is a unique and interactive museum dedicated to science, art, and human perception. Founded in 1969 by physicist Frank Oppenheimer, the Exploratorium has become a beloved institution, renowned for its hands-on exhibits and innovative approach to learning.

The museum's mission is to create inquiry-based experiences that transform learning worldwide. With over 650 interactive exhibits, the Exploratorium encourages visitors of all ages to explore the natural world, test scientific principles, and engage with artistic concepts. The exhibits cover a wide range of topics, including physics, biology, social behavior, and environmental science.

One of the most popular areas of the Exploratorium is the Tactile Dome, a dark maze that visitors navigate using their sense of touch. This immersive experience challenges perceptions and highlights the importance of sensory information in understanding the world. Another highlight is the Outdoor Gallery, which features exhibits that interact with the natural environment of the San Francisco Bay, including wind, tides, and sunlight.

The Exploratorium also offers a range of educational programs and workshops for students, educators, and families. These programs include science camps, teacher training sessions, and after-school activities designed to foster a love of learning and scientific curiosity. The museum's commitment to education extends beyond its walls, with initiatives that support science learning in schools and communities around the globe.

The museum's location at Pier 15 offers stunning views of the Bay Bridge and the waterfront, providing a scenic backdrop for exploration. The Exploratorium Café, run by local food purveyor Loretta Keller, offers a variety of delicious and sustainable food options, making it a perfect spot to relax and recharge.

The Exploratorium is more than just a museum; it is a vibrant learning laboratory that continually evolves to incorporate new scientific discoveries and artistic expressions. Whether you're a curious child, a science enthusiast, or someone seeking a unique and engaging experience, the Exploratorium offers a dynamic environment that inspires wonder and exploration.

Asian Art Museum

The Asian Art Museum, located in the Civic Center district of San Francisco, is one of the most comprehensive museums in the world dedicated to Asian art and culture. Housed in a beautifully renovated Beaux-Arts building that once served as the city's main library, the museum's vast collection and innovative exhibitions offer a deep dive into the rich and diverse artistic traditions of Asia.

Founded in 1966, the museum's collection spans over 6,000 years of history and includes more than 18,000 objects. These range from ancient archaeological artifacts to contemporary works of art, representing countries and cultures across Asia, including China, Japan, Korea, India, Southeast Asia, and the Himalayas. The collection encompasses a wide variety of mediums, such as painting, sculpture, ceramics, textiles, and decorative arts.

One of the museum's standout features is its collection of Chinese art, which includes rare jade carvings, intricate textiles, and stunning ceramics. Highlights include a Ming dynasty Buddha, a Tang dynasty camel, and a collection of exquisite calligraphy and ink paintings. The museum also boasts an impressive array of Japanese art, including samurai armor, ukiyo-e prints, and tea ceremony utensils.

The Asian Art Museum is known for its dynamic and engaging exhibitions, which explore both historical and contemporary themes. Recent exhibitions have focused on topics such as the influence of Asian art on Western culture, the role of women in Asian societies, and the intersection of tradition and modernity in contemporary Asian art. These exhibitions often feature multimedia installations, interactive elements, and works by living artists, offering a fresh and relevant perspective on Asian art and culture.

In addition to its permanent collection and rotating exhibitions, the museum offers a robust schedule of public programs and events. These include lectures, film screenings, performances, and hands-on workshops that provide deeper insights into Asian art and culture. The museum's educational initiatives extend to school programs and teacher resources, supporting the integration of Asian art into K-12 curricula.

The Asian Art Museum also features a delightful café and a well-curated museum store, offering a range of books, jewelry, and unique gifts inspired by the museum's collection.

The Asian Art Museum is a cultural gem that provides a comprehensive and immersive experience of Asia's artistic heritage. Whether you're a seasoned art aficionado or a curious visitor, the museum offers a rich and rewarding journey through the vast and diverse world of Asian art.

Contemporary Jewish Museum

The Contemporary Jewish Museum (CJM), located in the heart of downtown San Francisco, is a vibrant cultural institution dedicated to exploring contemporary perspectives on Jewish culture, history, art, and identity. Since its opening in 2008, the museum has become a dynamic space for artistic expression, dialogue, and community engagement.

Designed by renowned architect Daniel Libeskind, the museum's striking building is a work of art in itself. The design incorporates elements of traditional Jewish symbolism with contemporary architectural forms. The building's exterior features bold blue steel panels and a dramatic geometric shape that has become an iconic part of San Francisco's architectural landscape. Inside, the museum's open and flexible spaces provide an ideal setting for diverse exhibitions and public programs.

The Contemporary Jewish Museum's mission is to make the diversity of the Jewish experience relevant for a 21st-century audience. The museum achieves this through a wide range of exhibitions that explore Jewish themes, often in dialogue with broader cultural and social issues. The exhibitions feature works by contemporary artists, historical artifacts, multimedia installations, and interactive displays, offering multiple entry points for engagement and reflection.

Past exhibitions at CJM have covered a broad spectrum of topics, including the history of Jewish immigration to America, the contributions of Jewish artists to modern art movements, and the exploration of identity and memory in Jewish culture. These exhibitions often incorporate works by both Jewish and non-Jewish artists, fostering a rich and inclusive dialogue.

In addition to its exhibitions, the Contemporary Jewish Museum offers a robust schedule of public programs, including lectures, film screenings, performances, and workshops. These programs provide opportunities for visitors to engage with the themes and ideas presented in the exhibitions, often featuring artists, scholars, and community leaders as guest speakers.

The museum's educational initiatives are designed to reach a wide audience, from school groups to adult learners. The CJM offers guided tours, curriculum resources for teachers, and family-friendly activities that encourage exploration and creativity. The museum's commitment to accessibility and inclusivity is reflected in its diverse programming and welcoming environment.

The Contemporary Jewish Museum also features a café and a museum store that offers a curated selection of books, art, and unique gifts related to Jewish culture and contemporary art.

The Contemporary Jewish Museum is more than just a repository of artifacts; it is a lively and engaging space that invites visitors to explore the intersections of Jewish culture and contemporary life. Whether you're interested in art, history, or cultural dialogue, the CJM provides a thought-provoking and enriching experience in the heart of San Francisco.

The Walt Disney Family Museum

The Walt Disney Family Museum, located in the Presidio of San Francisco, is a tribute to the life and legacy of Walt Disney, the visionary creator of Mickey Mouse, Disneyland, and countless beloved animated films. Opened in 2009, the museum was founded by Walt Disney's daughter, Diane Disney Miller, to celebrate her father's extraordinary contributions to entertainment and popular culture.

Housed in a historic red-brick building, the museum features ten permanent galleries that chronologically detail Walt Disney's life, from his early days in Kansas City and Hollywood to the creation of his iconic characters and theme parks. The exhibits are richly illustrated with original drawings, animation cells, family photographs, and personal artifacts, offering an intimate and comprehensive look at Disney's creative journey.

One of the museum's highlights is the model of Disneyland, which showcases the park as it appeared during Walt Disney's lifetime, complete with detailed miniatures of iconic attractions. Another notable exhibit is the collection of over 200 awards that Disney received throughout his career, including his 22 Academy Awards.

The museum's interactive displays and multimedia presentations provide an engaging experience for visitors of all ages. These include rare film clips, early animation tests, and interviews with Disney and his collaborators. The exhibits not only highlight Disney's successes but also delve into the challenges and setbacks he faced, providing a balanced and inspiring narrative.

In addition to its permanent exhibits, the Walt Disney Family Museum hosts rotating special exhibitions that explore various aspects of Disney's legacy and the broader world of animation and storytelling. These exhibitions often feature works by contemporary artists and animators, connecting Disney's innovations to the present and future of the medium.

The museum also offers a range of educational programs, including workshops, lectures, and film screenings. These programs are designed to inspire creativity and innovation, reflecting Disney's enduring impact on the arts and entertainment.

The Walt Disney Family Museum's scenic location in the Presidio provides stunning views of the Golden Gate Bridge and San Francisco Bay, adding to the overall visitor experience. The museum's café and store offer Disney-themed refreshments and merchandise, making it a perfect destination for families and Disney enthusiasts.

The Walt Disney Family Museum is not just a celebration of one man's achievements but a testament to the power of imagination and perseverance. Whether you're a lifelong Disney fan or new to his story, the museum offers a rich and immersive experience that captures the magic of Walt Disney's world.

Museum of the African Diaspora

The Museum of the African Diaspora (MoAD), located in the Yerba Buena Arts District of San Francisco, is a dynamic cultural institution dedicated to celebrating the rich history, art, and cultural contributions of people of African descent worldwide. Since its opening in 2005, MoAD has become a vital space for exploring the diverse experiences and artistic expressions of the African diaspora.

MoAD's mission is to connect all people through the celebration and exploration of the art, culture, and history of the African diaspora. The museum achieves this through a wide range of exhibitions, public programs, and educational initiatives that highlight the global impact of African cultures and the ongoing contributions of the African diaspora to the arts and society.

The museum's exhibitions are known for their depth and diversity, featuring works by contemporary artists alongside historical artifacts and multimedia installations. These exhibitions often explore themes such as identity, migration, resilience, and the interconnections between Africa and the rest of the world. Notable past exhibitions have included works by artists such as Wangechi Mutu, Romare Bearden, and Kehinde Wiley, as well as thematic shows on topics like Afrofuturism and the Harlem Renaissance.

One of MoAD's standout features is its commitment to showcasing emerging and mid-career artists of African descent. Through its Emerging Artists Program, the museum provides a platform for new voices in contemporary art, supporting the development and recognition of diverse artistic talents.

MoAD also offers a robust schedule of public programs designed to engage and educate visitors of all ages. These include artist talks, film screenings, panel discussions, and performances that explore the cultural and historical contexts of the African diaspora. The museum's educational initiatives extend to school programs, family workshops, and community partnerships, fostering a deeper understanding of the African diaspora's contributions to global culture.

The museum's location in the Yerba Buena Arts District places it at the heart of San Francisco's cultural scene, alongside institutions such as the San Francisco Museum of Modern Art and the Contemporary Jewish Museum. This vibrant setting enhances the visitor experience, offering a rich cultural tapestry to explore.

MoAD's commitment to diversity, education, and artistic excellence makes it a vital cultural hub in San Francisco. Whether you're interested in contemporary art, historical exploration, or cultural dialogue, the Museum of the African Diaspora offers a thought-provoking and enriching experience that highlights the enduring influence of the African diaspora.

Legion of Honor

The Legion of Honor, located in San Francisco's scenic Lincoln Park, is a prestigious fine arts museum that showcases an impressive collection of European art, ancient artifacts, and decorative arts. The museum, officially known as the Fine Arts Museums of San Francisco, is housed in a stunning Beaux-Arts building designed as a replica of the Palais de la Légion d'Honneur in Paris. Since its opening in 1924, the Legion of Honor has been a cultural landmark, offering visitors a rich and immersive artistic experience.

The museum's collection spans over 4,000 years of art history, featuring works from the ancient Mediterranean, European paintings, sculpture, and decorative arts. Highlights include masterpieces by artists such as Rembrandt, Rubens, Monet, Degas, and Rodin. The museum's collection of Rodin sculptures is particularly notable, with "The Thinker" prominently displayed at the entrance, welcoming visitors to the museum.

The Legion of Honor's galleries are elegantly arranged, providing a serene and contemplative environment for viewing art. The museum's European paintings collection is a standout, with significant works from the Renaissance to the early 20th century. The collection includes works by El Greco, Vermeer, and Goya, as well as an extensive array of Impressionist and Post-Impressionist paintings.

In addition to its European art, the Legion of Honor features a remarkable collection of ancient art, including Egyptian, Greek, and Roman artifacts. These pieces offer a fascinating glimpse into the artistic and cultural achievements of ancient civilizations. The museum also houses an impressive collection of decorative arts, including fine porcelain, tapestries, and furniture, reflecting the craftsmanship and artistry of different historical periods.

The Legion of Honor is also renowned for its rotating special exhibitions, which bring world-class art to San Francisco. These exhibitions cover a wide range of topics and artistic movements, often featuring loans from major museums and private collections around the world. Recent exhibitions have explored themes such as Impressionism, Baroque art, and the connections between art and fashion.

The museum's location in Lincoln Park offers breathtaking views of the Golden Gate Bridge, the Pacific Ocean, and the surrounding parklands. The picturesque setting enhances the visitor experience, providing a peaceful and inspiring backdrop for art appreciation. The museum's café and gift shop offer a delightful selection of refreshments and unique gifts, making a visit to the Legion of Honor a complete and enriching experience.

The Legion of Honor's commitment to artistic excellence, historical preservation, and public engagement makes it a must-visit destination for art lovers and cultural enthusiasts. Whether you're exploring its extensive collections, attending a special exhibition, or simply enjoying the stunning views, the Legion of Honor provides a profound and memorable cultural experience in San Francisco.

San Francisco Cable Car Museum

The San Francisco Cable Car Museum, located in the Nob Hill neighborhood, is a fascinating destination that offers a deep dive into the history and mechanics of the city's iconic cable car system. Established in 1974, the museum is housed in the historic Washington-Mason cable car barn and powerhouse, which is still in operation today. This unique setting allows visitors to witness firsthand the inner workings of the cable car system that has been a vital part of San Francisco's transportation network since the late 19th century.

The museum's exhibits provide a comprehensive overview of the development and evolution of cable cars. It features a collection of historic cable cars, including the "Grip Car" No. 8, which dates back to the 1870s. These beautifully restored vehicles offer a tangible connection to the past, allowing visitors to appreciate the craftsmanship and engineering that went into their construction.

One of the highlights of the museum is the viewing platform that overlooks the powerhouse machinery. Here, visitors can see the massive winding wheels and cables that keep the system running. The sight and sound of the moving cables provide a vivid illustration of how the cable car system operates, pulling the cars up and down San Francisco's steep hills.

The museum also features informative displays on the history of the cable car system, including its invention by Andrew Smith Hallidie in 1873 and the role it played in shaping the city's development. Photographs, maps, and historical artifacts help to tell the story of how cable cars survived the 1906 earthquake and fire and continue to be a cherished symbol of San Francisco.

In addition to its historical exhibits, the museum offers educational programs and resources for visitors of all ages. These include guided tours, lectures, and interactive displays that explain the physics and mechanics behind cable car operation. The museum's gift shop offers a variety of souvenirs, including books, postcards, and cable car-themed merchandise.

The San Francisco Cable Car Museum is more than just a repository of artifacts; it is a living museum that celebrates the ingenuity and resilience of a transportation system that has become an integral part of the city's identity. Whether you're a history buff, an engineering enthusiast, or simply curious about this unique mode of transport, the Cable Car Museum provides an engaging and informative experience.

Cartoon Art Museum

The Cartoon Art Museum, located in the heart of San Francisco, is a unique cultural institution dedicated to the celebration and preservation of cartoon art in all its forms. Established in 1984, the museum offers a diverse range of exhibits and programs that highlight the artistic and cultural significance of cartoons, comics, and animation.

The museum's collection spans a wide array of styles and genres, from classic newspaper comic strips and superhero comics to contemporary graphic novels and animated films. Visitors can explore the works of legendary cartoonists such as Charles Schulz, creator of "Peanuts," and modern innovators like Raina Telgemeier, known for her best-selling graphic novels. The exhibits provide a fascinating look at the evolution of cartoon art and its impact on popular culture.

One of the standout features of the Cartoon Art Museum is its rotating exhibitions, which showcase both historical and contemporary works. These exhibitions often focus on specific themes, artists, or genres, offering visitors a deep dive into different aspects of cartoon art. Past exhibitions have covered topics such as the history of animation, the role of comics in social justice movements, and the artistic process behind creating a graphic novel.

In addition to its exhibits, the museum offers a variety of educational programs and workshops for visitors of all ages. These include cartooning classes, animation workshops, and lectures by industry professionals. The museum's commitment to education extends to its school outreach programs, which aim to inspire creativity and literacy through the medium of cartoon art.

The Cartoon Art Museum also features a comprehensive research library, housing a vast collection of books, magazines, and original artwork. This resource is invaluable for scholars, students, and enthusiasts interested in studying the history and techniques of cartoon art.

The museum's location in a vibrant cultural district enhances the visitor experience, offering easy access to other attractions and amenities. The museum store provides a selection of unique gifts, books, and memorabilia related to cartoon art, making it a great place to find something special for fans of all ages.

The Cartoon Art Museum is a testament to the enduring appeal and artistic value of cartoons and comics. By celebrating the work of past and present artists, the museum provides a dynamic and engaging space for appreciating the creativity and cultural significance of this beloved art form.

Beat Museum

The Beat Museum, located in the North Beach neighborhood of San Francisco, is a tribute to the influential Beat Generation, a group of writers, poets, and artists who revolutionized American literature and culture in the 1950s and 1960s. Founded by Jerry Cimino in 2003, the museum is dedicated to preserving the legacy of the Beats and inspiring new generations to explore their own creativity and self-expression.

The museum's collection includes an extensive array of artifacts, memorabilia, and original works associated with key figures of the Beat Generation, such as Jack Kerouac, Allen Ginsberg, William S. Burroughs, and Neal Cassady. Visitors can explore first editions of seminal works like Kerouac's "On the Road" and Ginsberg's "Howl," as well as personal letters, photographs, and original manuscripts that provide insight into the lives and creative processes of these iconic writers.

One of the highlights of the Beat Museum is its collection of rare and personal items, including Kerouac's typewriter, Ginsberg's personal journals, and photographs capturing the Beats' travels and gatherings. These artifacts offer a tangible connection to the Beat Generation, allowing visitors to delve deeper into the personal histories and cultural impact of these literary pioneers.

The museum also features a series of informative exhibits that contextualize the Beats within the broader social and cultural movements of their time. These exhibits explore themes such as the Beats' influence on the counterculture of the 1960s, their contributions to the civil rights and anti-war movements, and their lasting impact on contemporary literature and art.

In addition to its permanent collection, the Beat Museum hosts a variety of events, including poetry readings, film screenings, and book signings. These events often feature contemporary writers and artists who draw inspiration from the Beat ethos, creating a lively and interactive environment that fosters creative exchange and community engagement.

The Beat Museum's educational initiatives include workshops, lectures, and tours that provide deeper insights into the history and legacy of the Beat Generation. The museum's store offers a range of Beat-related merchandise, including books, posters, and memorabilia, making it a great place to find unique gifts for literary enthusiasts.

Situated in North Beach, an area historically associated with the Beat Generation, the museum is surrounded by other Beat landmarks such as City Lights Bookstore and Vesuvio Café. This vibrant cultural setting enhances the visitor experience, providing a sense of the neighborhood's rich literary history.

The Beat Museum is not just a place to learn about the past; it is a space that encourages visitors to embrace the spirit of the Beats by challenging convention and exploring their own creative potential. Whether you're a longtime fan of the Beat Generation or discovering their work for the first time, the Beat Museum offers a compelling and inspiring journey through the lives and legacies of these groundbreaking artists.

Mexican Museum

The Mexican Museum, located in San Francisco's vibrant Yerba Buena Gardens, is a cultural institution dedicated to celebrating the art, culture, and heritage of Mexico and the Mexican-American community. Founded in 1975 by artist Peter Rodriguez, the museum has grown to house an impressive collection of over 16,000 objects, representing thousands of years of Mexican and Latino art and culture.

The museum's collection spans pre-Hispanic, colonial, and contemporary periods, offering a comprehensive view of Mexican artistic traditions. Among its notable holdings are pre-Columbian artifacts, including ceramics, textiles, and sculptures that showcase the rich and diverse cultures that flourished in Mexico before the Spanish conquest. These artifacts provide valuable insights into the religious, social, and artistic practices of ancient civilizations such as the Aztec, Maya, and Olmec.

The colonial period is represented through religious and secular art, including paintings, sculptures, and decorative arts that illustrate the fusion of indigenous and European influences. This period of Mexican history is crucial in understanding the cultural and artistic evolution of the region, and the museum's collection highlights the intricate craftsmanship and unique stylistic developments of this era.

The museum also boasts an extensive collection of modern and contemporary Mexican and Chicano art. Works by renowned artists such as Diego Rivera, David Alfaro Siqueiros, and Rufino Tamayo are featured alongside those of contemporary Mexican-American artists, reflecting the ongoing dialogue between traditional and contemporary art forms. The museum actively supports emerging artists, providing a platform for new voices in the Latino art community.

In addition to its permanent collection, the Mexican Museum hosts rotating exhibitions that explore various aspects of Mexican and Latino culture. These exhibitions often address themes such as identity, migration, and social justice, providing a space for critical reflection and dialogue.

The Mexican Museum's educational programs are designed to engage visitors of all ages and backgrounds. These programs include workshops, lectures, and school tours that promote a deeper understanding and appreciation of Mexican art and culture. The museum also collaborates with community organizations to create culturally relevant programming that resonates with the local Mexican-American community.

The Mexican Museum is more than just a repository of art; it is a vibrant cultural hub that celebrates the rich tapestry of Mexican and Latino heritage. Whether you are interested in ancient artifacts, colonial art, or contemporary works, the Mexican Museum offers a rich and immersive experience that highlights the diversity and creativity of Mexican culture.

Randall Museum

The Randall Museum, nestled in the scenic Corona Heights Park in San Francisco, is a beloved community museum dedicated to inspiring creativity and fostering a love of science, nature, and the arts among visitors of all ages. Established in 1951, the museum offers a wide range of hands-on exhibits, educational programs, and live animal displays that make learning fun and engaging.

The museum's mission is to provide a dynamic environment where visitors can explore the natural world, understand the principles of science, and express themselves through the arts. Its exhibits are designed to be interactive and accessible, encouraging visitors to touch, explore, and experiment.

One of the highlights of the Randall Museum is its live animal exhibit, which features a variety of animals native to California, including birds of prey, reptiles, amphibians, and small mammals. These exhibits offer a close-up look at the diverse wildlife of the region and provide valuable lessons about animal behavior, habitat conservation, and environmental stewardship.

The museum also boasts a well-equipped science lab where visitors can participate in hands-on experiments and learn about topics such as physics, chemistry, and biology. The lab hosts regular workshops and classes that cater to children, families, and school groups, fostering a deeper understanding of scientific principles through practical, engaging activities.

The Randall Museum's art studios are another key attraction, offering classes and workshops in various artistic disciplines, including painting, ceramics, woodworking, and crafts. These programs are designed to nurture creativity and provide participants with the skills and confidence to express themselves artistically. The museum's gallery spaces showcase rotating exhibitions of artwork created by local artists and students, highlighting the vibrant artistic community in San Francisco.

The museum's model railroad exhibit is a favorite among visitors, featuring an intricate layout that depicts California's diverse landscapes and historical landmarks. This exhibit, maintained by the Golden Gate Model Railroad Club, provides an opportunity for visitors to learn about the history of railroads in California and the engineering behind model railroading.

In addition to its permanent exhibits and programs, the Randall Museum offers a variety of special events throughout the year, including science fairs, art shows, and seasonal festivals. These events provide opportunities for the community to come together, celebrate, and learn in a fun and supportive environment.

Surrounded by the natural beauty of Corona Heights Park, the Randall Museum also encourages outdoor exploration and appreciation of the natural world. The park's trails offer stunning views of San Francisco and serve as an extension of the museum's educational mission.

The Randall Museum is a cherished institution that offers a rich and diverse array of learning experiences. Whether you're interested in science, nature, or the arts, the museum provides a welcoming and stimulating environment that inspires curiosity and creativity in visitors of all ages.

Theaters and Performances

War Memorial Opera House

The War Memorial Opera House, located in San Francisco's Civic Center, is a stunning example of Beaux-Arts architecture and a cultural landmark that has been at the heart of the city's performing arts scene since it opened in 1932. Designed by architects Arthur Brown Jr. and G. Albert Lansburgh, the Opera House is part of the War Memorial and Performing Arts Center, which also includes the Herbst Theatre, the Davies Symphony Hall, and the Veterans Building.

The War Memorial Opera House is home to the San Francisco Opera, one of the most prestigious opera companies in the United States, and the San Francisco Ballet, the oldest professional ballet company in the country. Its majestic interior features a grand foyer, an elegant marble staircase, and richly decorated auditoriums with plush seating, offering an atmosphere of grandeur and refinement.

The Opera House's stage has hosted some of the world's most renowned opera singers, conductors, and dancers. Its acoustics and design are meticulously crafted to provide an exceptional experience for both performers and audiences. The annual performance calendar is filled with a diverse range of productions, from classic operas by Verdi and Puccini to contemporary works and world premieres, as well as seasonal ballet performances including the beloved "Nutcracker."

In addition to its regular performances, the War Memorial Opera House is also a venue for various cultural events, concerts, and special occasions. The building itself is a historic site, having played a significant role in international history; it was the site of the signing of the United Nations Charter in 1945.

The Opera House offers a range of amenities to enhance the visitor experience, including elegant bars and lounges where guests can enjoy refreshments during intermissions. Guided tours of the Opera House are available, providing insights into the building's history, architecture, and the behind-the-scenes workings of an opera and ballet production.

The War Memorial Opera House stands as a testament to San Francisco's dedication to the arts and its commitment to preserving cultural heritage.

Whether you are a seasoned opera aficionado, a ballet enthusiast, or a newcomer to the performing arts, the Opera House provides a breathtaking setting to enjoy world-class performances in the heart of San Francisco.

Orpheum Theatre

The Orpheum Theatre, located on Market Street in San Francisco, is one of the city's most iconic and historic performance venues. Built in 1926, the Orpheum was designed by renowned architect B. Marcus Priteca and is a prime example of the Beaux-Arts style with its grand façade and opulent interior. The theatre's design includes intricate plasterwork, ornate chandeliers, and a stunning ceiling mural, creating an atmosphere of timeless elegance.

Originally part of the Orpheum Circuit, a chain of vaudeville theaters, the Orpheum Theatre has evolved over the decades to host a wide variety of performances, including Broadway shows, concerts, and special events. The theatre's location in the vibrant Civic Center district makes it easily accessible and a key player in San Francisco's cultural scene.

One of the Orpheum Theatre's defining features is its versatility and ability to accommodate large-scale productions. The stage has hosted numerous acclaimed Broadway shows, such as "Hamilton," "The Lion King," "Wicked," and "Les Misérables." These productions have drawn large audiences and contributed to the theatre's reputation as a premier destination for top-tier entertainment.

The Orpheum Theatre is managed by BroadwaySF, which oversees several of San Francisco's major theaters. This affiliation ensures a steady stream of high-quality performances and helps maintain the theatre's historic charm and modern amenities. The Orpheum's seating capacity of approximately 2,200 allows for an intimate yet grand viewing experience, with excellent sightlines and acoustics enhancing the enjoyment of every performance.

In addition to Broadway productions, the Orpheum Theatre hosts concerts, comedy shows, and other special events, making it a versatile venue that appeals to a wide range of tastes. The theatre's rich history and architectural beauty make it a popular spot for both locals and tourists.

Visitors to the Orpheum Theatre can also enjoy the convenience of nearby dining and entertainment options, making it easy to plan a full evening out in San Francisco's bustling downtown area. Whether you're attending a blockbuster Broadway show or a one-night-only concert, the Orpheum Theatre offers a memorable and immersive cultural experience.

Curran Theatre

The Curran Theatre, located in the heart of San Francisco's Theater District on Geary Street, is a historic and beloved venue that has been a cornerstone of the city's performing arts scene since it opened in 1922. Designed by architect Arthur Brown Jr., who also designed San Francisco City Hall, the Curran boasts a rich history and a legacy of hosting some of the most celebrated theatrical productions.

The theatre's elegant interior features an opulent lobby, grand staircases, and a beautifully adorned auditorium with a seating capacity of approximately 1,600. The Curran's design is a blend of Italian Renaissance and French Baroque styles, with intricate detailing and plush seating that create a luxurious and intimate atmosphere for theatergoers.

Throughout its history, the Curran Theatre has been home to numerous legendary productions, including the original San Francisco runs of "My Fair Lady," "The Phantom of the Opera," "Les Misérables," and "A Chorus Line." The theatre's stage has seen performances by some of the biggest names in theatre and entertainment, solidifying its reputation as a premier destination for high-caliber productions.

In 2015, the Curran Theatre underwent a major renovation under the leadership of Tony Award-winning producer Carole Shorenstein Hays. The renovation modernized the theatre's facilities while preserving its historic charm, resulting in a state-of-the-art venue that continues to attract top-tier performances. The updated Curran features enhanced acoustics, improved seating, and modern amenities that elevate the overall theatre experience.

The Curran Theatre is known for its commitment to presenting innovative and diverse productions. Its programming includes a mix of Broadway hits, cutting-edge new works, and unique special events. The theatre has also established itself as a platform for groundbreaking and experimental performances, providing a space for artists to push the boundaries of traditional theatre.

In addition to its main stage productions, the Curran Theatre offers various educational and community programs designed to engage and inspire audiences of all ages. These initiatives include talkbacks, workshops, and special events that foster a deeper connection between the performers and the community.

Located in the bustling Union Square area, the Curran Theatre is surrounded by a vibrant array of dining, shopping, and entertainment options, making it a perfect destination for a night out in San Francisco. Whether you're a seasoned theatergoer or experiencing live theatre for the first time, the Curran Theatre offers an unforgettable experience that celebrates the magic of the performing arts.

American Conservatory Theater (A.C.T.)

The American Conservatory Theater (A.C.T.) is a cornerstone of San Francisco's vibrant performing arts scene, known for its high-quality productions and commitment to theater education. Founded in 1965 by William Ball, A.C.T. has grown into one of the leading regional theaters in the United States, with a mission to nurture the art of live theater through dynamic productions and comprehensive training programs.

A.C.T. operates out of the historic Geary Theater, a stunning Beaux-Arts building located in the heart of San Francisco's Theater District. The Geary Theater, which originally opened in 1910, was meticulously restored after being severely damaged in the 1989 Loma Prieta earthquake. The 1,040-seat theater combines old-world charm with modern amenities, providing an intimate and elegant setting for performances.

A.C.T.'s diverse repertoire includes classic plays, contemporary works, and world premieres. The theater is renowned for its bold and innovative productions, which often incorporate cutting-edge technology and new interpretations of classic texts. Past productions have featured works by Shakespeare, Anton Chekhov, and Tennessee Williams, as well as contemporary playwrights like Tom Stoppard, Sam Shepard, and David Mamet.

In addition to its mainstage productions, A.C.T. is dedicated to developing new talent through its renowned Master of Fine Arts (M.F.A.) program. The program, which is one of the most respected graduate theater training programs in the country, offers rigorous training in acting, directing, and production. Graduates of the program have gone on to successful careers in theater, film, and television.

A.C.T. also runs the Young Conservatory, a training program for aspiring actors aged 8-19. This program provides young people with the opportunity to develop their skills and perform in professional-quality productions.

A.C.T. is deeply committed to community engagement and offers a range of educational programs and initiatives designed to make theater accessible to all. These include audience enrichment programs, such as post-show discussions and lectures, as well as outreach programs that bring theater education to local schools and community centers.

The American Conservatory Theater is not just a venue for performances but a vital cultural institution that enriches the San Francisco community. Whether you are attending a performance, participating in a workshop, or studying in one of its training programs, A.C.T. offers a profound and inspiring theatrical experience.

Golden Gate Theatre

The Golden Gate Theatre, located on Market Street in San Francisco, is a historic and beloved performance venue that has been a major part of the city's cultural landscape since its opening in 1922. Designed by renowned architect G. Albert Lansburgh, the theater originally served as a vaudeville house before transitioning to a movie palace and eventually becoming a premier destination for live theater and Broadway shows.

The Golden Gate Theatre's architecture is a stunning example of the opulent and ornate style of early 20th-century theaters. Its grand façade features intricate terra cotta detailing, while the interior boasts a lavish lobby with marble columns, crystal chandeliers, and rich decorative elements. The main auditorium, with its elegant proscenium arch and plush seating, provides an intimate and immersive experience for theatergoers.

The theater's seating capacity of approximately 2,300 makes it one of the largest venues in San Francisco, capable of hosting large-scale productions. Over the years, the Golden Gate Theatre has presented a wide array of performances, from classic plays and musicals to concerts and special events. It is particularly well-known for hosting touring Broadway shows, bringing top-tier productions to the Bay Area.

Notable productions that have graced the Golden Gate Theatre's stage include "Hamilton," "The Book of Mormon," "Wicked," and "Les Misérables." The theater's programming is managed by BroadwaySF, which ensures a steady lineup of high-quality shows that appeal to diverse audiences.

The Golden Gate Theatre's central location on Market Street places it in the heart of San Francisco's cultural district, making it easily accessible by public transportation. The theater's proximity to numerous dining and entertainment options makes it an ideal destination for a night out in the city.

In addition to its regular performances, the Golden Gate Theatre offers a range of amenities to enhance the visitor experience. These include comfortable seating, state-of-the-art sound and lighting systems, and a variety of concessions and bars. The theater also provides special accommodations for patrons with disabilities, ensuring that everyone can enjoy the magic of live theater.

The Golden Gate Theatre is a cherished landmark that combines historical elegance with modern entertainment. Whether you are a seasoned theater enthusiast or a first-time visitor, the Golden Gate Theatre offers a memorable and enchanting experience that showcases the best of San Francisco's performing arts.

San Francisco Symphony

The San Francisco Symphony, founded in 1911, is one of the most respected and innovative orchestras in the world. Based at the Louise M. Davies Symphony Hall in the Civic Center district, the Symphony is renowned for its exceptional musicianship, diverse programming, and commitment to community engagement and music education.

Davies Symphony Hall, designed by architects Skidmore, Owings & Merrill and opened in 1980, is a modern, acoustically superb venue that seats over 2,700 patrons. The hall's sleek design and state-of-the-art acoustics create an ideal environment for both musicians and audiences, enhancing the overall concert experience.

Under the artistic leadership of Music Director Esa-Pekka Salonen, the San Francisco Symphony presents a wide range of concerts that span classical masterpieces, contemporary works, and innovative new commissions. The Symphony's repertoire includes symphonies, concertos, chamber music, and choral works, featuring compositions from the Baroque era to the present day. The Symphony is also known for its adventurous programming, often incorporating multimedia elements and collaborations with artists from various disciplines.

The San Francisco Symphony's commitment to new music is exemplified by its commissioning and performing of works by contemporary composers. The Symphony's adventurous spirit has led to numerous world premieres and critically acclaimed recordings. Its discography includes Grammy Award-winning recordings of works by Mahler, John Adams, and many others.

In addition to its regular concert series, the San Francisco Symphony offers a variety of special events and community programs. These include the popular "Film with Live Orchestra" series, holiday concerts, and the "SoundBox" series, which presents eclectic performances in a nightclub-style setting. The Symphony also engages with the community through free concerts, outreach programs, and partnerships with local schools and organizations.

The Symphony's education programs are designed to inspire and educate young musicians and audiences. These programs include the acclaimed "Adventures in Music" program for elementary school students, the "Youth Orchestra" for talented young musicians, and the "Music for Families" series, which introduces families to the joys of orchestral music.

The San Francisco Symphony's dedication to excellence, innovation, and community engagement makes it a cornerstone of the city's cultural life. Whether you are attending a classical concert, a contemporary performance, or a special event, the San Francisco Symphony offers an enriching and inspiring musical experience that resonates with audiences of all ages.

SFJAZZ Center

The SFJAZZ Center, located in San Francisco's vibrant Hayes Valley neighborhood, is a premier venue dedicated to the celebration and performance of jazz music. Opened in 2013, the SFJAZZ Center is the first freestanding building in the United States designed specifically for jazz performance and education, solidifying San Francisco's position as a major hub for jazz enthusiasts.

Designed by award-winning architect Mark Cavagnero, the SFJAZZ Center is a modern, state-of-the-art facility that combines sleek, contemporary design with superb acoustics. The building features multiple performance spaces, including the main Robert N. Miner Auditorium, which seats up to 700 guests in an intimate, acoustically pristine environment. The Joe Henderson Lab, a smaller venue within the center, offers a more casual and intimate setting for performances, workshops, and community events.

The SFJAZZ Center hosts a wide array of concerts featuring both renowned and emerging artists from the world of jazz. Its programming spans a diverse range of jazz styles, from traditional and swing to bebop, fusion, and avant-garde. Notable performers who have graced the stage include Herbie Hancock, Wynton Marsalis, Esperanza Spalding, and Chick Corea, among many others. The center's commitment to presenting high-quality performances has made it a beloved destination for jazz aficionados and newcomers alike.

In addition to its robust concert schedule, SFJAZZ is deeply committed to music education and community outreach. The center offers a variety of educational programs designed to engage and inspire students of all ages. These include the SFJAZZ High School All-Stars, a pre-professional program for talented young musicians, and the Family Matinee Series, which introduces children and families to the world of jazz through interactive performances. The center also offers workshops, masterclasses, and lectures led by prominent jazz artists and educators.

The SFJAZZ Center's location in the heart of Hayes Valley places it within walking distance of numerous dining, shopping, and cultural attractions, making it an ideal destination for an evening out. The center's café and bar provide a welcoming space for patrons to enjoy refreshments before or after performances, further enhancing the overall experience.

SFJAZZ's innovative design, exceptional acoustics, and dedication to artistic excellence make it a cornerstone of San Francisco's cultural landscape. Whether you're attending a concert, participating in an educational program, or simply exploring the center, SFJAZZ offers a dynamic and enriching experience that celebrates the spirit and evolution of jazz music.

The Fillmore

The Fillmore, located in the Western Addition neighborhood of San Francisco, is one of the most iconic and historic music venues in the United States. Known for its rich musical heritage and intimate atmosphere, The Fillmore has played a pivotal role in shaping the city's vibrant live music scene since its opening in 1912.

Originally a dance hall, The Fillmore gained national prominence in the 1960s under the management of legendary concert promoter Bill Graham. During this era, the venue became a hub for the burgeoning counterculture movement and hosted performances by some of the most influential artists of the time. The Fillmore's stage saw legendary acts such as Jimi Hendrix, Janis Joplin, The Grateful Dead, and Jefferson Airplane, solidifying its reputation as a premier destination for live music.

The Fillmore's architecture and interior design contribute to its unique charm and allure. The venue features a classic marquee, ornate chandeliers, and a balcony that provides excellent sightlines for concertgoers. The walls are adorned with vintage concert posters, creating a nostalgic ambiance that honors the venue's storied past. The Fillmore's relatively small capacity of about 1,250 ensures an intimate concert experience, allowing audiences to feel a close connection with the performers.

Today, The Fillmore continues to attract top-tier talent from a wide range of musical genres, including rock, jazz, blues, hip-hop, and electronic music. The venue's eclectic programming reflects its commitment to presenting both established and emerging artists, ensuring that each concert offers a unique and memorable experience.

One of The Fillmore's enduring traditions is the distribution of free apples to concertgoers, a practice that dates back to the venue's early days under Bill Graham's management. This quirky custom adds to the venue's distinctive character and enhances the overall concert experience.

In addition to its regular concert schedule, The Fillmore hosts special events, private parties, and community gatherings, further cementing its role as a cultural hub in San Francisco. The venue's central location makes it easily accessible, with a variety of dining and entertainment options nearby, allowing patrons to enjoy a full night out in the city.

The Fillmore's legacy of musical innovation, intimate atmosphere, and commitment to providing exceptional live music experiences make it a cherished landmark in San Francisco. Whether you're a longtime fan or a first-time visitor, a night at The Fillmore promises to be an unforgettable journey through the rich tapestry of live music history.

Great American Music Hall

The Great American Music Hall, nestled in San Francisco's Tenderloin district, is one of the city's oldest and most revered music venues. Established in 1907, the venue boasts a rich history and a timeless charm that continues to attract music lovers and performers from around the world.

The Great American Music Hall's architecture is a stunning example of early 20th-century design, featuring ornate balconies, marble columns, and intricate frescoes that create an atmosphere of elegance and grandeur. The venue's opulent interior, complete with a gilded ceiling and sparkling chandeliers, offers a unique and intimate setting for live performances. With a seating capacity of approximately 470, the hall provides an up-close and personal experience, allowing audiences to connect deeply with the artists on stage.

Throughout its long history, the Great American Music Hall has hosted an impressive array of talent spanning various musical genres, including rock, jazz, blues, folk, and indie. The venue has welcomed legendary acts such as Duke Ellington, Sarah Vaughan, Van Morrison, and more contemporary artists like Arcade Fire, The White Stripes, and Patti Smith. This eclectic programming reflects the hall's commitment to showcasing diverse musical talent and providing unforgettable live music experiences.

The Great American Music Hall is known for its excellent acoustics, which ensure that every performance sounds clear and immersive. The venue's layout, with its tiered seating and spacious dance floor, offers great views and an enjoyable experience for all attendees, whether they prefer to stand and dance or sit and enjoy the show.

In addition to its regular concert schedule, the Great American Music Hall hosts a variety of special events, including private parties, corporate events, and community gatherings. The venue's historic charm and versatile space make it an ideal location for memorable occasions.

The Great American Music Hall's location in the vibrant Tenderloin district places it within walking distance of numerous dining and entertainment options, making it a convenient and appealing destination for a night out in San Francisco. The venue also offers a full-service bar and a menu featuring a selection of food and beverages, allowing patrons to enjoy a complete evening of entertainment and refreshment.

The Great American Music Hall's combination of historic elegance, superb acoustics, and diverse programming make it a beloved landmark in San Francisco's music scene. Whether you're attending a concert by a legendary artist or discovering new talent, the Great American Music Hall offers a magical and intimate setting that celebrates the joy of live music.

Historic Sites

Mission San Francisco de Asís (Mission Dolores)

Mission San Francisco de Asís, commonly known as Mission Dolores, is the oldest surviving structure in San Francisco and one of the most historically significant sites in California. Founded on June 29, 1776, by Lieutenant José Joaquin Moraga and Father Francisco Palou, the mission was named for Saint Francis of Assisi and the nearby creek, Arroyo de los Dolores.

Mission Dolores is a testament to the early Spanish colonial history and the Franciscan missionary efforts in California. The original adobe mission church, completed in 1791, has withstood earthquakes and the passage of time, making it the oldest intact building in San Francisco. The adjacent basilica, built in the early 20th century, stands as a striking example of Mission Revival architecture, complementing the historic mission.

Visitors to Mission Dolores can explore the well-preserved mission church, which features thick adobe walls, a timbered roof, and original redwood logs. The interior is adorned with historic religious artifacts, including statues, paintings, and altarpieces that reflect the mission's Spanish and Native American heritage. The adjacent cemetery is the only remaining cemetery within San Francisco city limits, where notable early settlers and Native Americans are buried.

The mission's museum offers a deeper insight into the history and daily life of the mission, showcasing artifacts, documents, and exhibits on the interactions between the Spanish missionaries and the indigenous Ohlone people. The museum also highlights the mission's role in the broader context of California's mission system.

Mission Dolores remains an active parish, serving the local community with regular religious services and cultural events. The site also hosts educational programs and tours for visitors of all ages, providing an opportunity to learn about California's colonial past and the legacy of the Franciscan missions.

Mission Dolores is not only a historical landmark but also a place of reflection and cultural significance. Whether you're interested in history, architecture, or spirituality, a visit to Mission Dolores offers a rich and immersive experience that connects you to the early roots of San Francisco and the enduring influence of its mission heritage.

Fort Mason

Fort Mason, located on the northern waterfront of San Francisco, is a historic site that has evolved from a military post into a vibrant cultural and recreational hub. Established in 1864 as a coastal defense site, Fort Mason played a significant role in military operations, particularly during World War II, when it served as a major embarkation point for troops and supplies heading to the Pacific Theater.

Today, Fort Mason is part of the Golden Gate National Recreation Area and is known for its stunning views of the Golden Gate Bridge, Alcatraz Island, and the San Francisco Bay. The site encompasses a variety of historical buildings, green spaces, and cultural institutions, making it a popular destination for both locals and tourists.

One of the key attractions at Fort Mason is the Fort Mason Center for Arts & Culture, a dynamic venue that hosts a wide range of artistic and cultural events. The center includes galleries, theaters, and event spaces that feature performances, exhibitions, and workshops in disciplines such as visual arts, theater, dance, and literature. The annual San Francisco International Arts Festival is among the many notable events held at the Fort Mason Center, attracting artists and audiences from around the world.

Fort Mason is also home to several museums and historical sites, including the Museo Italo Americano, which celebrates Italian-American heritage, and the San Francisco Maritime National Historical Park Visitor Center, which offers exhibits on the city's maritime history. The park's historic buildings, such as the General's Residence and the Officers' Club, provide a glimpse into the fort's military past and are available for tours and private events.

The green spaces and waterfront areas at Fort Mason offer ample opportunities for outdoor recreation. Visitors can enjoy picnicking, walking, and cycling along the scenic pathways, or simply relax and take in the panoramic views. The Great Meadow, a large open lawn, is a popular spot for picnics, kite flying, and outdoor festivals.

Fort Mason also features a variety of dining options, from casual cafes to fine dining restaurants, many of which offer spectacular views of the bay. The site's Farmers' Market, held on Sundays, is a favorite among locals for fresh produce, artisanal foods, and community gatherings.

Fort Mason's blend of historical significance, cultural vibrancy, and natural beauty makes it a unique and multifaceted destination. Whether you're exploring its museums, attending an arts event, or enjoying the outdoor spaces, Fort Mason offers a rich and engaging experience that highlights the diverse heritage and dynamic spirit of San Francisco.

Maritime National Historical Park

The San Francisco Maritime National Historical Park, located at the western end of Fisherman's Wharf, is a treasure trove of maritime history and a beloved destination for visitors interested in the rich seafaring heritage of San Francisco. Established in 1988, the park preserves and interprets the maritime history of the Pacific Coast, offering a unique and immersive experience through its historic ships, museum, and waterfront areas.

One of the park's main attractions is its impressive collection of historic vessels, docked at Hyde Street Pier. These ships include the Balclutha, a 19th-century square-rigged sailing ship that once transported goods around Cape Horn; the Eureka, a steam-powered ferryboat that served San Francisco Bay commuters; and the C.A. Thayer, a schooner that was used for both lumber and fishing. Visitors can explore these well-preserved ships, each of which offers a glimpse into the life and work of sailors and maritime workers from different eras.

The park's Visitor Center, located across the street from Hyde Street Pier, features exhibits and displays that provide an in-depth look at San Francisco's maritime history. The center includes models, photographs, and artifacts that tell the stories of the city's bustling waterfront, the development of its shipping industry, and the diverse communities that contributed to its maritime heritage.

Adjacent to the Visitor Center is the Maritime Museum, housed in a stunning Streamline Moderne building that was originally constructed as a bathhouse in the 1930s. The museum's exhibits cover a wide range of topics, from the Gold Rush and the age of sail to modern maritime innovations. One of the highlights is the museum's collection of intricately detailed ship models, which illustrate the evolution of ship design and construction.

The park also features the Aquatic Park Historic District, a picturesque area that includes a sandy beach, a lagoon, and a municipal pier. This area provides a scenic backdrop for picnicking, swimming, and enjoying views of the bay and the Golden Gate Bridge. The park's location along the waterfront makes it an ideal spot for a leisurely stroll or a bike ride along the Bay Trail.

Throughout the year, the San Francisco Maritime National Historical Park hosts a variety of educational programs, including ranger-led tours, boat-building workshops, and maritime skills demonstrations. These programs offer hands-on learning opportunities and bring the history of the park to life for visitors of all ages.

The San Francisco Maritime National Historical Park is a unique and enriching destination that celebrates the city's deep connection to the sea. Whether you're exploring the historic ships, visiting the museum, or enjoying the waterfront, the park offers a captivating experience that highlights the enduring legacy of San Francisco's maritime past.

Presidio of San Francisco

The Presidio of San Francisco is a vast and historically significant park located at the northern tip of the San Francisco Peninsula. Once a military post dating back to 1776, the Presidio is now a major part of the Golden Gate National Recreation Area and a beloved destination for its natural beauty, cultural attractions, and recreational opportunities.

The Presidio's rich history spans several centuries, beginning as a Spanish fort before transitioning to Mexican control and ultimately becoming a key U.S. Army base. It played a vital role in various military conflicts, including the Mexican-American War, the Civil War, and World War II. The Presidio was decommissioned as an active military base in 1994 and transferred to the National Park Service, which has since worked to preserve its historical legacy while transforming it into a public park.

One of the most striking features of the Presidio is its stunning landscapes, which include forested areas, rolling hills, and scenic overlooks with breathtaking views of the Golden Gate Bridge, San Francisco Bay, and the Pacific Ocean. The park offers a network of hiking and biking trails, such as the popular Coastal Trail and the Presidio Promenade, providing visitors with ample opportunities to explore its diverse ecosystems and enjoy outdoor activities.

The Presidio is home to several cultural and historical sites that offer insights into its storied past. The Presidio Officers' Club, one of San Francisco's oldest buildings, serves as a museum and cultural center with exhibits on the history of the Presidio and rotating art displays. The Walt Disney Family Museum, located in the park, celebrates the life and legacy of Walt Disney with an extensive collection of memorabilia and interactive exhibits.

Art enthusiasts can explore the Presidio's public art installations, including the striking "Spire" and "Wood Line" sculptures by artist Andy Goldsworthy, which seamlessly integrate with the natural landscape. The park also features the beautifully restored Main Post, a central hub with historic buildings, grassy lawns, and the visitor center, where guests can learn more about the Presidio's history and attractions.

The Presidio's recreational offerings are diverse, with golf courses, sports fields, and picnic areas available for public use. Crissy Field, a former airfield turned waterfront park, is a favorite spot for walking, jogging, and kite flying, with its scenic trails and sandy beach.

The Presidio is also a hub for dining and hospitality, with several restaurants, cafes, and hotels located within the park. Visitors can enjoy a meal with a view at the Presidio Social Club or the Commissary, both offering delicious cuisine in historic settings.

The Presidio of San Francisco is a unique blend of natural beauty, historical significance, and cultural richness. Whether you're hiking its trails, exploring its museums, or simply taking in the views, the Presidio offers a multifaceted experience that highlights the best of San Francisco's past and present.

Angel Island

Angel Island, often referred to as the "Ellis Island of the West," is a historical and natural treasure located in San Francisco Bay. As the largest island in the bay, it offers a rich blend of history, cultural significance, and natural beauty, making it a popular destination for both locals and tourists.

Historically, Angel Island served several important roles. During the Civil War, it was a military installation for the Union Army. From 1910 to 1940, the island was the site of the Angel Island Immigration Station, where hundreds of thousands of immigrants, primarily from China, were processed and detained under harsh conditions due to the restrictive Chinese Exclusion Act. Today, the Immigration Station has been restored as a museum and memorial, providing visitors with poignant insights into the immigrant experience and the challenges faced by those seeking new lives in America.

The island is also home to several historic military installations, including Fort McDowell, used for processing soldiers during World Wars I and II, and Nike Missile sites from the Cold War era. Guided tours and exhibits across the island offer fascinating glimpses into these periods of American history.

In addition to its historical significance, Angel Island is renowned for its natural beauty and recreational opportunities. The island features numerous hiking and biking trails that offer stunning views of San Francisco, the Golden Gate Bridge, Marin County, and Mount Tamalpais. The most popular trail, a 5-mile loop around the island, provides panoramic vistas and access to historical sites.

Picnicking, wildlife viewing, and camping are also popular activities on Angel Island. The island's diverse ecosystems, including grasslands, woodlands, and coastal scrub, support a variety of wildlife, making it a haven for nature enthusiasts. The island's visitor center offers educational displays about the island's natural and cultural history.

Accessible by ferry from San Francisco, Tiburon, and Oakland, Angel Island provides an ideal day trip or overnight getaway. The combination of rich history, scenic beauty, and recreational opportunities makes Angel Island a must-visit destination in the San Francisco Bay Area.

Fort Funston

Fort Funston, located on the southwestern coast of San Francisco, is a beloved recreational area known for its dramatic cliffs, scenic vistas, and unique natural features. Originally a military fortification, Fort Funston is now part of the Golden Gate National Recreation Area, offering visitors a stunning coastal experience.

The area is characterized by its towering sand dunes and rugged cliffs that provide breathtaking views of the Pacific Ocean. These cliffs are a popular spot for hang gliding, and Fort Funston is considered one of the premier hang gliding locations in the United States. Experienced gliders can be seen soaring above the cliffs, taking advantage of the strong coastal winds and panoramic views.

Fort Funston is also a haven for dog owners, as it is one of the few places in San Francisco where dogs are allowed to roam off-leash. The expansive, sandy trails and open spaces provide ample room for dogs to explore and play, making it a favorite destination for pet lovers.

Hiking and horseback riding are popular activities at Fort Funston, with trails that wind through coastal scrub and dune habitats. The Sunset Trail is particularly notable, offering a relatively easy hike with stunning ocean views. Along the way, visitors can encounter a variety of wildlife, including raptors, shorebirds, and native plant species that thrive in the coastal environment.

The beach at Fort Funston, accessible via a steep trail, offers a more secluded and rugged coastal experience compared to other San Francisco beaches. The strong currents and waves make it less suitable for swimming, but it is an excellent spot for beachcombing, picnicking, and enjoying the natural beauty of the coastline.

In addition to its recreational opportunities, Fort Funston has a rich military history. During World War II, it was part of the coastal defense system, housing artillery batteries designed to protect San Francisco Bay from enemy ships. Remnants of these fortifications, including bunkers and gun emplacements, can still be seen today, adding a historical dimension to the natural landscape.

Fort Funston's combination of dramatic scenery, recreational activities, and historical significance makes it a unique and cherished part of the San

Francisco Bay Area. Whether you're looking to hike, glide, or simply take in the ocean views, Fort Funston offers a memorable coastal experience.

Balclutha Ship

The Balclutha, a historic three-masted, steel-hulled sailing ship, is a centerpiece of the San Francisco Maritime National Historical Park. Built in 1886 in Glasgow, Scotland, the Balclutha is one of the few remaining tall ships from the 19th century and offers a fascinating glimpse into the era of maritime trade and exploration.

Originally designed for the grain trade, the Balclutha sailed between Europe and the west coast of North America, often rounding the treacherous Cape Horn. The ship's sturdy construction and impressive sail plan made it well-suited for long voyages across rough seas. Over the years, the Balclutha also carried various cargoes, including lumber and salmon, as it traversed the Pacific Ocean.

Today, the Balclutha is permanently docked at Hyde Street Pier in San Francisco, where it serves as a museum ship. Visitors can explore the ship's decks and interiors, gaining insight into the life of sailors during the Age of Sail. The meticulously restored cabins, galley, and cargo holds offer a vivid portrayal of the daily routines, hardships, and adventures experienced by the crew.

One of the highlights of a visit to the Balclutha is the opportunity to climb the rigging and experience the ship from the perspective of a sailor working high above the deck. The panoramic views of San Francisco Bay from the ship's masts are breathtaking and provide a unique vantage point for photography and appreciation of the surrounding maritime landscape.

The Balclutha's educational programs and guided tours delve into the ship's history, construction, and the broader context of maritime trade in the late 19th and early 20th centuries. The ship also hosts living history events, where reenactors in period costume bring the past to life through demonstrations and storytelling.

In addition to its role as a museum, the Balclutha is part of a larger collection of historic vessels at Hyde Street Pier, which includes the ferryboat Eureka, the schooner C.A. Thayer, and the steam tug Hercules.

Together, these ships provide a comprehensive overview of San Francisco's rich maritime heritage.

The Balclutha's preservation as a museum ship ensures that future generations can continue to learn about and appreciate the history of maritime trade and the enduring legacy of the Age of Sail. A visit to the Balclutha offers a captivating journey back in time, making it an essential destination for history buffs, maritime enthusiasts, and anyone interested in San Francisco's nautical past.

Haas-Lilienthal House

The Haas-Lilienthal House, located in the Pacific Heights neighborhood of San Francisco, is a beautifully preserved example of Victorian architecture and a significant cultural landmark. Built in 1886 for William Haas, a prominent businessman, the house has remained largely unchanged, offering a rare glimpse into the domestic life of San Francisco's elite during the late 19th and early 20th centuries.

Designed by architect Peter R. Schmidt in the Queen Anne style, the Haas-Lilienthal House features ornate detailing, gabled roofs, and a distinctive corner tower. The exterior is adorned with intricate woodwork, including decorative brackets, spindles, and patterned shingles, showcasing the craftsmanship and architectural flair of the period.

The interior of the house is equally impressive, with richly detailed wood paneling, stained glass windows, and period furnishings that reflect the opulence and elegance of the Victorian era. Visitors can explore the various rooms, including the formal parlor, dining room, and bedrooms, each meticulously decorated to convey the lifestyle and tastes of the Haas family.

One of the unique aspects of the Haas-Lilienthal House is its status as the only Victorian house in San Francisco that is open to the public as a museum. Operated by San Francisco Heritage, a preservation organization, the house offers guided tours that provide insights into the history of the family, the architectural features of the house, and the broader historical context of San Francisco during the Victorian and Edwardian periods.

The house's original fixtures and furnishings have been preserved, allowing visitors to experience the home much as it would have appeared over a century ago. Highlights include the elegant dining room with its hand-carved sideboard, the cozy library with a collection of vintage books, and the upstairs bedrooms with period-appropriate decor.

In addition to regular tours, the Haas-Lilienthal House hosts various events and educational programs, including lectures, workshops, and special tours that delve deeper into aspects of Victorian life and architecture. The house also serves as a venue for private events, offering a unique and historic setting for gatherings and celebrations.

The Haas-Lilienthal House is more than just a museum; it is a living testament to San Francisco's architectural and cultural heritage. Its preservation and continued use as an educational resource ensure that the history and beauty of the Victorian era remain accessible to the public. A visit to the Haas-Lilienthal House offers a captivating journey into the past, highlighting the architectural splendor and historical significance of one of San Francisco's most treasured landmarks.

Observation Decks and Scenic Views

Golden Gate Bridge Vista Point

The Golden Gate Bridge Vista Point, located at the northern end of the iconic Golden Gate Bridge in Marin County, offers one of the most breathtaking views in the San Francisco Bay Area. This popular lookout provides visitors with an unparalleled perspective of the bridge, the San Francisco skyline, and the surrounding natural beauty of the bay and the Marin Headlands.

The vista point is easily accessible by car, bike, or on foot, making it a convenient stop for tourists and locals alike. Ample parking is available, though it can fill up quickly during peak times, so early arrival is recommended. For those arriving by bike or on foot, the journey across the Golden Gate Bridge itself is a memorable experience, offering stunning views at every turn.

From the vista point, visitors can enjoy panoramic views of the Golden Gate Bridge's striking orange towers set against the backdrop of the sparkling blue waters of the bay and the rugged hills of Marin County. On clear days, the vista point offers a perfect vantage for photographing the bridge, Alcatraz Island, Angel Island, and the distant skyline of San Francisco.

The vista point is equipped with several amenities to enhance the visitor experience. Informational plaques provide historical context and interesting facts about the construction and significance of the Golden Gate Bridge. There are also viewing telescopes available, allowing for a closer look at the bridge and the surrounding landmarks.

In addition to the stunning vistas, the area around the vista point offers opportunities for outdoor recreation. Nearby trails, such as the Coastal Trail, offer scenic hiking and biking routes that showcase the natural beauty of the Marin Headlands and the coastline.

The Golden Gate Bridge Vista Point is not just a spot for sightseeing; it also serves as a reminder of the engineering marvel that is the Golden Gate Bridge. Opened in 1937, the bridge was the longest suspension bridge in the world at the time and remains an iconic symbol of San Francisco and American ingenuity.

Whether you're a first-time visitor or a long-time resident, the Golden Gate Bridge Vista Point offers a must-see experience that captures the grandeur and beauty of one of the world's most famous landmarks. The breathtaking views and the opportunity to witness the majesty of the Golden Gate Bridge up close make this a destination not to be missed.

Coit Tower Observation Deck

Perched atop Telegraph Hill in San Francisco, Coit Tower is an iconic landmark known for its stunning 360-degree views of the city and the bay. Built in 1933 and named after Lillie Hitchcock Coit, a wealthy socialite and patron of the city's firefighters, the tower stands as a tribute to the city's colorful history and offers visitors a unique perspective of San Francisco.

The Art Deco tower rises 210 feet above the city and is constructed of unpainted reinforced concrete. Its cylindrical shape and sleek design make it a distinctive feature of the San Francisco skyline. The tower is part of Pioneer Park, a lovely green space that offers its own scenic vistas and a peaceful retreat from the bustling city below.

Visitors to Coit Tower can access the observation deck via an elevator that ascends through the tower's core. From the top, the observation deck provides breathtaking views in all directions. To the north, you can see Alcatraz Island and the Golden Gate Bridge, while to the west lies the expanse of the Pacific Ocean. The Financial District, the Bay Bridge, and the distant hills of Marin County are also visible, making it an ideal spot for panoramic photography.

One of the unique aspects of Coit Tower is its collection of murals that adorn the interior walls of the ground floor. These murals were painted by various artists as part of a Public Works of Art Project during the Great Depression and depict scenes of contemporary life in California. The murals are a vibrant and historically significant feature, offering insights into the social and economic conditions of the 1930s.

The surrounding neighborhood of Telegraph Hill is a charming area with steep streets and historic homes, adding to the allure of a visit to Coit Tower. The climb to the tower can be an adventure in itself, with steps and paths winding through lush gardens and offering occasional glimpses of the views to come.

Coit Tower is accessible by car, with limited parking available, but many visitors choose to walk or take public transportation due to the challenging parking situation. The Filbert Steps and the Greenwich Steps are two popular routes for pedestrians, offering a scenic and invigorating climb to the top.

A visit to the Coit Tower Observation Deck provides not only an opportunity to see some of the best views in San Francisco but also a chance to connect with the city's artistic and cultural heritage. Whether you're a history buff, an art lover, or simply someone who appreciates a great view, Coit Tower offers a memorable experience that encapsulates the essence of San Francisco.

Twin Peaks Overlook

Twin Peaks Overlook is one of San Francisco's most spectacular vantage points, offering panoramic views of the city, the bay, and beyond. Located near the geographic center of the city, Twin Peaks consists of two prominent hills—Eureka Peak and Noe Peak—rising about 922 feet above sea level. This elevation provides visitors with unobstructed, breathtaking vistas that capture the diverse and dynamic landscape of San Francisco.

The drive to Twin Peaks Overlook is an adventure in itself, with winding roads that ascend through residential neighborhoods and parklands. Once at the top, visitors are greeted with a stunning 360-degree view that encompasses downtown San Francisco, the Golden Gate Bridge, the Bay Bridge, Alcatraz Island, and the distant hills of Marin County. On clear days, the view extends as far as the East Bay and the Pacific Ocean, making it a favorite spot for photographers and sightseers.

The overlook is equipped with viewing platforms and telescopes, allowing for closer inspection of the city's landmarks and natural features. Informational plaques provide context and interesting facts about the geography and history of the area, enhancing the visitor experience.

One of the most remarkable aspects of Twin Peaks Overlook is its accessibility. The site is open year-round and is easily reached by car, with ample parking available at the summit. For those who prefer a more active approach, hiking and biking trails wind their way up the hills, offering a rewarding way to reach the top while enjoying the natural beauty of the area.

The overlook is particularly popular at sunrise and sunset when the light casts a magical glow over the city, creating perfect conditions for stunning photographs and memorable experiences. The sight of the city lights twinkling at night is equally captivating, providing a romantic and serene backdrop for evening visits.

Twin Peaks Overlook is also an excellent spot for birdwatching and wildlife observation. The natural habitats around the peaks support a variety of species, making it a peaceful retreat for nature enthusiasts.

In addition to its scenic beauty, Twin Peaks has a cultural and historical significance for San Francisco. The area has been preserved as part of the Twin Peaks Natural Area, ensuring that its natural state remains protected for future generations to enjoy.

Whether you're a local resident or a visitor to San Francisco, a trip to Twin Peaks Overlook offers an unparalleled view of the city and its surroundings. The combination of stunning vistas, accessibility, and natural beauty makes it a must-visit destination for anyone looking to experience the best of what San Francisco has to offer.

de Young Museum Observation Tower

The de Young Museum Observation Tower, located in San Francisco's Golden Gate Park, offers one of the most breathtaking panoramic views of the city. Part of the renowned de Young Museum, the observation tower is a must-visit attraction that provides a unique perspective of San Francisco's diverse landscape and iconic landmarks.

The de Young Museum, originally founded in 1895 and redesigned by the architectural firm Herzog & de Meuron, reopened in 2005 with its new, modern look. The observation tower, also known as the Hamon Tower, rises 144 feet above the park, making it one of the highest vantage points in the area. The tower's distinctive design features a twisted, perforated copper facade that not only gives it a striking appearance but also allows natural light to filter through, creating a dynamic interplay of light and shadow inside.

Access to the observation tower is included with museum admission, and a high-speed elevator whisks visitors to the top floor. The tower's glass-walled observation deck offers unobstructed, 360-degree views of San

Francisco and beyond. From this vantage point, visitors can see the Golden Gate Bridge, the Pacific Ocean, the Marin Headlands, downtown San Francisco, and the lush expanses of Golden Gate Park itself. The sightlines extend to the surrounding neighborhoods, providing a comprehensive view of the city's varied topography.

The observation tower is not just about the view; it also offers a peaceful and contemplative space away from the bustling galleries below. The serene atmosphere makes it an ideal spot for reflection and appreciation of the natural and urban landscapes. Informational panels along the walls of the observation deck provide context and details about the landmarks visible from the tower, enhancing the educational experience.

The de Young Museum itself is home to a vast collection of American art, textiles, and international contemporary art, making it one of the premier cultural institutions in San Francisco. A visit to the museum, combined with the experience of the observation tower, provides a well-rounded cultural and aesthetic experience.

The de Young Museum Observation Tower is an architectural marvel and a highlight of any visit to Golden Gate Park. Whether you're a local resident or a tourist, the tower offers an unparalleled view of San Francisco's beauty and complexity, making it a memorable part of the museum experience.

The View Lounge at Marriott Marquis

The View Lounge, perched atop the Marriott Marquis in downtown San Francisco, offers one of the most stunning panoramic views of the city's skyline. Located on the 39th floor of the iconic hotel, The View Lounge is a popular destination for both locals and visitors looking to enjoy sophisticated cocktails and breathtaking scenery in an elegant setting.

The lounge's design maximizes its prime location with expansive floor-to-ceiling windows that provide unobstructed views of San Francisco. As guests enter, they are greeted by a sweeping vista that includes iconic landmarks such as the Transamerica Pyramid, the Bay Bridge, and the bustling streets of the Financial District. The ambiance is further enhanced by the lounge's modern decor, featuring sleek furnishings, warm lighting, and an inviting atmosphere that encourages relaxation and socializing.

The View Lounge is renowned for its creative and expertly crafted cocktails. The menu includes a wide selection of signature drinks that highlight local ingredients and seasonal flavors. Whether you prefer a classic martini, a refreshing mojito, or a unique concoction inspired by the city's diverse culinary scene, the skilled bartenders at The View Lounge can deliver a memorable drink experience. The lounge also offers an extensive wine list and a variety of local craft beers, ensuring that there is something to suit every palate.

In addition to its impressive drink menu, The View Lounge features a selection of delectable small plates and appetizers. Guests can enjoy dishes such as artisan cheese platters, savory flatbreads, and gourmet sliders, all designed to complement the beverage offerings and enhance the overall dining experience.

The View Lounge is not just a place to enjoy a drink; it is a destination for special occasions and memorable moments. The lounge frequently hosts live music and themed events, providing a lively and dynamic atmosphere that attracts a diverse crowd. Whether you're celebrating a milestone, meeting friends for a night out, or simply unwinding after a long day, The View Lounge offers an unparalleled setting to do so.

With its breathtaking views, exceptional cocktails, and elegant ambiance, The View Lounge at the Marriott Marquis stands out as one of San Francisco's premier destinations for elevated nightlife. The combination of stunning scenery and refined hospitality makes it a must-visit spot for anyone looking to experience the best of what the city has to offer from high above its bustling streets.

Neighborhood Exploration

North Beach

North Beach, often referred to as San Francisco's "Little Italy," is a vibrant and historic neighborhood known for its rich cultural heritage, lively nightlife, and culinary delights. Nestled between Chinatown and Fisherman's Wharf, North Beach offers a unique blend of old-world charm and modern urban energy.

The heart of North Beach is Washington Square Park, a popular gathering spot surrounded by notable landmarks such as Saints Peter and Paul Church. This iconic church, with its twin spires, has been a central part of the neighborhood's identity and a backdrop for many community events and festivals.

One of North Beach's main attractions is its thriving dining scene. The neighborhood is dotted with classic Italian restaurants, cafes, and bakeries that have been family-run for generations. Institutions like Tony's Pizza Napoletana, known for its award-winning pies, and Caffe Trieste, a historic coffeehouse that was a favorite haunt of Beat Generation writers, offer a taste of the area's rich culinary history.

Speaking of the Beat Generation, North Beach was a pivotal center for this literary movement in the 1950s and 60s. Landmarks like City Lights Bookstore, founded by poet Lawrence Ferlinghetti, and Vesuvio Cafe, a bohemian bar frequented by Jack Kerouac and Allen Ginsberg, remain popular destinations for literature enthusiasts and cultural tourists alike.

In addition to its historical and cultural significance, North Beach boasts a vibrant nightlife. The area is home to a variety of bars, jazz clubs, and live music venues that come alive after dark. The famous Beach Blanket Babylon, a long-running musical revue known for its outrageous costumes and satirical humor, has entertained audiences for decades and is a must-see for visitors.

North Beach's charm also lies in its picturesque streets and unique architecture. The neighborhood's hills provide stunning views of the city and the bay, while its colorful Victorian homes and quaint alleyways invite leisurely exploration.

Overall, North Beach offers a delightful mix of history, culture, and entertainment. Whether you're indulging in Italian cuisine, tracing the footsteps of literary greats, or enjoying the vibrant nightlife, North Beach provides a quintessential San Francisco experience that captures the city's diverse and dynamic spirit.

Haight-Ashbury

Haight-Ashbury, famously known as the epicenter of the 1960s counterculture movement, is a neighborhood that exudes a unique blend of historic significance and bohemian charm. Located at the intersection of Haight and Ashbury streets, this vibrant area is synonymous with the Summer of Love, a time when thousands of young people flocked to San Francisco in search of peace, love, and artistic expression.

The neighborhood's history is palpable as you stroll down Haight Street, where colorful Victorian houses stand as reminders of the area's past. Many of these buildings have been meticulously preserved, showcasing the ornate architecture that defines San Francisco's historic charm. The Red Victorian, a historic hotel turned community hub, is just one example of the neighborhood's commitment to preserving its cultural heritage.

Haight-Ashbury's streets are lined with an eclectic mix of vintage clothing stores, record shops, bookstores, and unique boutiques. Amoeba Music, housed in a former bowling alley, is one of the largest independent music stores in the world and a haven for vinyl enthusiasts. The neighborhood's shopping scene reflects its diverse and alternative spirit, offering everything from rare records to retro fashion.

Cafes and restaurants in Haight-Ashbury cater to a wide range of tastes, from vegan and vegetarian eateries to classic diners and international cuisine. The area's culinary diversity ensures that there is something for everyone, whether you're looking for a hearty breakfast, a quick snack, or a gourmet dinner.

Haight-Ashbury's cultural significance is further highlighted by its connection to iconic musicians and artists. The Grateful Dead, Janis Joplin, and Jefferson Airplane all lived and performed in the neighborhood during the 1960s. Today, visitors can explore landmarks such as the Red House, where the Grateful Dead once lived, and the former site of the Straight Theater, a legendary performance venue.

The neighborhood also offers a variety of green spaces and parks. Nearby Golden Gate Park provides a tranquil escape with its expansive gardens, museums, and recreational facilities. The smaller but equally charming Buena Vista Park offers panoramic views of the city and the bay, making it a perfect spot for a relaxing afternoon.

Haight-Ashbury remains a symbol of San Francisco's free-spirited and artistic culture. Whether you're exploring its historic sites, browsing its unique shops, or simply soaking in the vibrant atmosphere, Haight-Ashbury offers a fascinating journey through one of the most iconic neighborhoods in the city.

The Mission District

The Mission District, often simply referred to as "The Mission," is one of San Francisco's oldest and most culturally diverse neighborhoods. Named after Mission San Francisco de Asís (Mission Dolores), the oldest surviving structure in the city, this area is a vibrant tapestry of history, art, and culinary delights.

At the heart of the Mission District is Mission Dolores Park, a beloved green space that attracts locals and tourists alike. The park offers stunning views of the San Francisco skyline and is a popular spot for picnics, sunbathing, and people-watching. On weekends, the park buzzes with activity, hosting everything from yoga classes to impromptu music performances.

The Mission is renowned for its rich Latino heritage, which is vividly reflected in its culinary scene. The neighborhood is home to some of the city's best Mexican and Central American cuisine, with taquerias and pupuserias lining the streets. La Taqueria, famous for its burritos, and El Farolito, known for its tacos, are just a couple of the many eateries that draw food enthusiasts from all over.

Murals are a defining feature of the Mission District, with vibrant artwork adorning buildings, alleyways, and public spaces. Balmy Alley and Clarion Alley are two must-visit locations where the walls come alive with colorful, politically charged murals created by local artists. These murals often reflect the neighborhood's history, social issues, and cultural pride, making the Mission an open-air gallery that tells the story of its community.

Valencia Street is the commercial heart of the Mission, offering an eclectic mix of boutiques, bookstores, cafes, and bars. The street is known for its independent shops and unique finds, from vintage clothing at Afterlife to the latest literary releases at Dog Eared Books. The nightlife on Valencia Street is equally diverse, with venues like The Chapel and the Latin American Club offering live music, craft cocktails, and a lively atmosphere.

The Mission District also has a burgeoning arts scene, with numerous galleries and performance spaces showcasing local talent. The Roxie Theater, the oldest continuously operating cinema in the city, screens independent films and documentaries, adding to the neighborhood's cultural vibrancy.

The Mission District's blend of historic landmarks, culinary excellence, artistic expression, and community spirit make it a dynamic and captivating part of San Francisco. Whether you're savoring a delicious meal, exploring vibrant murals, or enjoying a sunny day in the park, the Mission offers an authentic and enriching experience that reflects the soul of the city.

Nob Hill

Nob Hill, one of San Francisco's most upscale and historically significant neighborhoods, is synonymous with luxury, elegance, and breathtaking views. Perched high above the city, Nob Hill has long been a symbol of San Francisco's wealth and sophistication, offering a unique blend of historic landmarks, upscale dining, and cultural attractions.

The neighborhood's history dates back to the late 19th century when it became the preferred residential area for the city's wealthiest citizens, known as the "Big Four" – Leland Stanford, Mark Hopkins, Collis P. Huntington, and Charles Crocker. These railroad magnates built grand mansions atop the hill, setting the tone for Nob Hill's opulent character.

One of the most iconic landmarks in Nob Hill is the Fairmont San Francisco, a historic luxury hotel that has hosted countless celebrities, dignitaries, and events since it opened in 1907. The hotel's grandeur, stunning architecture, and panoramic views make it a must-visit destination. Nearby, the InterContinental Mark Hopkins hotel, another historic gem, offers the renowned Top of the Mark lounge, where guests can enjoy cocktails while taking in sweeping views of the city and the bay.

Grace Cathedral, an architectural marvel, is another centerpiece of Nob Hill. This stunning Gothic Revival cathedral, completed in 1964, features magnificent stained glass windows, intricate mosaics, and a labyrinth for meditation. The cathedral is not only a place of worship but also a cultural hub, hosting concerts, art exhibits, and community events.

Nob Hill is also home to Huntington Park, a charming green space that provides a peaceful retreat amid the bustling city. The park features beautifully landscaped gardens, a playground, and the striking Fountain of the Tortoises, making it a favorite spot for locals and visitors to relax and enjoy the scenery.

For dining and nightlife, Nob Hill offers an array of upscale restaurants and sophisticated bars. The Big 4 Restaurant, located in the Huntington Hotel, provides a classic San Francisco dining experience with its elegant decor and refined menu. Meanwhile, the Tonga Room & Hurricane Bar, situated in the Fairmont Hotel, offers a unique tropical-themed experience with live music and exotic cocktails.

Nob Hill's central location and elevation provide some of the best views in the city. The historic cable cars that run through the neighborhood offer a nostalgic and scenic way to explore the area, connecting Nob Hill to other key parts of San Francisco, such as Union Square and Fisherman's Wharf.

With its rich history, architectural splendor, and luxurious ambiance, Nob Hill is a quintessential San Francisco neighborhood. Whether you're exploring its historic landmarks, enjoying a fine dining experience, or simply taking in the panoramic views, Nob Hill offers a timeless and elegant escape in the heart of the city.

Japantown

Japantown, also known as Nihonmachi, is one of San Francisco's most culturally rich and vibrant neighborhoods. Established in the early 1900s, Japantown is one of only three remaining Japantowns in the United States, offering a unique and immersive experience into Japanese culture and heritage.

Centered around the Japan Center, a shopping and cultural complex that spans several city blocks, Japantown is a bustling hub of activity. The Japan Center, with its iconic Peace Pagoda—a five-tiered concrete structure gifted by San Francisco's sister city, Osaka—serves as the neighborhood's focal point. The complex is home to a variety of shops, restaurants, and cultural institutions, all of which provide a taste of Japan right in the heart of San Francisco.

The culinary scene in Japantown is a highlight, offering a wide range of Japanese cuisine. From traditional sushi and ramen to contemporary fusion dishes, the neighborhood's eateries cater to all tastes. Popular spots include Sushi Ran, known for its fresh and innovative sushi, and Hinodeya Ramen Bar, which serves authentic ramen in a cozy setting. Additionally, the area is famous for its sweet treats, such as mochi and taiyaki, available at local dessert shops and cafes.

Japantown's cultural offerings extend beyond its cuisine. The neighborhood hosts numerous events and festivals throughout the year, celebrating Japanese traditions and culture. The Cherry Blossom Festival, held every April, is one of the most anticipated events, featuring parades, performances, and traditional crafts. The Nihonmachi Street Fair, another popular event, showcases the neighborhood's vibrant community through music, food, and art.

The cultural institutions in Japantown provide further insights into Japanese heritage. The Japanese Cultural and Community Center of Northern California (JCCCNC) offers classes and workshops in traditional arts, such as calligraphy and tea ceremony, while the nearby National Japanese American Historical Society preserves and shares the history of Japanese Americans in the Bay Area.

Japantown's unique blend of history, culture, and modern amenities makes it a must-visit destination in San Francisco. Whether you're exploring its bustling shops, savoring delicious Japanese cuisine, or participating in cultural events, Japantown offers a rich and immersive experience that celebrates the enduring legacy of Japanese culture in America.

Castro District

The Castro District, commonly known as "The Castro," is one of San Francisco's most iconic and historically significant neighborhoods, renowned for its vibrant LGBTQ+ community and rich cultural heritage. Located in the heart of the city, The Castro is a symbol of pride, activism, and diversity, offering visitors a unique and welcoming atmosphere.

The Castro's history as an LGBTQ+ haven dates back to the 1960s and 70s when it became a sanctuary for people seeking acceptance and community. The neighborhood's transformation was significantly influenced by Harvey Milk, the first openly gay elected official in California, whose leadership and activism left a lasting legacy. The Castro Theatre, a historic movie palace with a distinctive neon marquee, often hosts screenings and events celebrating LGBTQ+ culture, adding to the area's rich cultural tapestry.

Walking through The Castro, visitors will notice the vibrant rainbow flags that adorn the streets, symbolizing the neighborhood's inclusive spirit. The main thoroughfare, Castro Street, is lined with a diverse array of shops, cafes, bars, and restaurants that cater to all tastes. Iconic establishments like Twin Peaks Tavern, one of the first gay bars in the U.S. with open windows, and Hot Cookie, a beloved bakery, are must-visit spots that embody the neighborhood's friendly and eclectic vibe.

The Castro is also home to several important landmarks and cultural institutions. The GLBT Historical Society Museum, located on 18th Street, offers exhibits and archives that document the history and contributions of the LGBTQ+ community. The Pink Triangle Park and Memorial, a small but poignant garden, honors the memory of LGBTQ+ individuals persecuted during the Holocaust.

Throughout the year, The Castro hosts numerous events and celebrations that draw visitors from around the world. The annual San Francisco Pride Parade, one of the largest and most famous pride events globally, often features a vibrant procession through The Castro. Other notable events include the Castro Street Fair, a lively neighborhood festival celebrating the local community with music, art, and food.

The Castro District is not just a neighborhood; it is a symbol of resilience, activism, and pride. Whether you're exploring its historic sites, enjoying its vibrant nightlife, or simply soaking in the inclusive atmosphere, The Castro offers a unique and inspiring experience that celebrates the diversity and spirit of San Francisco.

Marina District

The Marina District is one of San Francisco's most picturesque and sought-after neighborhoods, known for its scenic waterfront views, upscale dining, and vibrant social scene. Located along the northern edge of the city, the Marina District offers a unique blend of natural beauty, historic charm, and modern amenities, making it a favorite destination for both locals and visitors.

One of the defining features of the Marina District is its stunning waterfront, with the Marina Green serving as the neighborhood's centerpiece. This expansive park offers sweeping views of the Golden Gate Bridge, Alcatraz Island, and the San Francisco Bay, providing an idyllic setting for picnics, jogging, cycling, and sailing. The Marina Green is a popular spot for outdoor activities and events, attracting fitness enthusiasts and families alike.

Adjacent to the Marina Green is the historic Palace of Fine Arts, an architectural gem originally constructed for the 1915 Panama-Pacific Exposition. The Palace, with its grand rotunda and tranquil lagoon, is one of San Francisco's most photographed landmarks. It serves as a cultural hub, hosting various events, exhibitions, and performances throughout the year.

The Marina District's commercial streets, particularly Chestnut Street, are lined with a diverse array of boutiques, cafes, restaurants, and bars. This bustling thoroughfare offers everything from high-end fashion and artisanal goods to casual dining and gourmet cuisine. Popular spots include A16, known for its exceptional Italian dishes and wine selection, and the Tipsy Pig, a lively gastropub with a great selection of craft beers and cocktails.

The neighborhood's vibrant nightlife scene is another draw, with numerous bars and lounges offering a lively atmosphere well into the night. Whether you're looking for a laid-back pub, a trendy cocktail bar, or a dance club, the Marina District has something to cater to every preference.

In addition to its recreational and dining offerings, the Marina District is home to several historical and cultural sites. The Fort Mason Center for Arts & Culture, a former military base turned cultural complex, hosts a variety of art exhibitions, performances, and community events. The center's scenic location along the waterfront adds to its appeal, making it a popular destination for both cultural and recreational activities.

The Marina District's combination of natural beauty, vibrant social scene, and rich cultural heritage makes it one of San Francisco's most desirable neighborhoods.

Food and Dining

Iconic San Francisco Foods

San Francisco is famous for its iconic foods, each deeply embedded in the city's culinary fabric and cultural identity. Sourdough bread, Dungeness crab, and Mission-style burritos are not just foods in San Francisco—they are institutions, beloved by locals and tourists alike. Each of these quintessential San Francisco eats has its own unique history and places to find the best versions in the city.

Sourdough Bread

San Francisco's sourdough bread is world-renowned, known for its tangy flavor and chewy texture. This distinct flavor is credited to the natural wild yeasts and bacteria present in the Bay Area, particularly Lactobacillus sanfranciscensis, which thrive in the region's climate.

Sourdough bread has been a staple in San Francisco since the Gold Rush era, when French bakers brought their techniques to the city. Over the years, it has become a symbol of San Francisco's culinary heritage. Traditional San Francisco sourdough is enjoyed on its own, as a sandwich base, or as a bread bowl for clam chowder.

Some of the most famous sourdough bakeries in San Francisco include:

- **Boudin Bakery:** Established in 1849, Boudin is a San Francisco institution known for its original sourdough bread recipe.
- **Tartine Bakery:** A modern favorite, Tartine offers a variety of artisanal breads, including their renowned sourdough loaves.
- **Acme Bread Company:** Located at the Ferry Building, Acme Bread Company provides high-quality sourdough and other baked goods.

Dungeness Crab

Dungeness crab is another culinary icon of San Francisco, celebrated for its sweet and tender meat. This local delicacy is typically harvested from November to June, marking a festive season for seafood lovers in the Bay Area.

The tradition of enjoying Dungeness crab dates back to the mid-19th century when Italian and Portuguese fishermen settled in the region. Today, Dungeness crab is often served cracked and cleaned, accompanied by melted butter or a tangy cocktail sauce.

Some of the best places to enjoy Dungeness crab in San Francisco include:

- **Fisherman's Wharf:** The heart of San Francisco's seafood scene, where you can find fresh Dungeness crab at various seafood stands and restaurants.
- **Swan Oyster Depot:** A historic seafood counter offering fresh, locally caught crab and other seafood delicacies.
- **Pier Market Seafood Restaurant:** Located at Pier 39, this restaurant is known for its fresh Dungeness crab dishes and scenic waterfront views.

Mission-Style Burritos

The Mission-style burrito is a beloved San Francisco staple, characterized by its large size and variety of fillings wrapped in a steamed flour tortilla. Originating in the Mission District, these burritos are typically packed with rice, beans, meat, salsa, guacamole, and sour cream.

The Mission-style burrito emerged in the 1960s, reflecting the vibrant Mexican-American culture of the Mission District. Today, it is a favorite meal for locals and visitors, known for its bold flavors and satisfying portions.

Some of the most celebrated taquerias for Mission-style burritos in San Francisco include:

- **La Taqueria:** A Mission District institution known for its delicious and generously filled burritos, voted as the best burrito in America by various food critics.

- **El Farolito:** Famous for its hearty and flavorful burritos, El Farolito is a go-to spot for late-night eats.
- **Taqueria Cancun:** Known for its vibrant atmosphere and delicious burritos, Taqueria Cancun is a favorite among locals.

Each of these iconic foods—sourdough bread, Dungeness crab, and Mission-style burritos—represents a slice of San Francisco's rich culinary history. Sampling these treats is not just about enjoying great food; it's about experiencing a piece of the city's vibrant culture and traditions.

Fine Dining

San Francisco is home to some of the world's most renowned fine dining establishments, offering exquisite culinary experiences that attract food enthusiasts from around the globe. The city's fine dining scene is characterized by its diversity, innovation, and the impressive number of Michelin-starred restaurants.

Michelin-Starred Restaurants

San Francisco boasts an impressive number of Michelin-starred restaurants, representing a wide array of cuisines and styles. These establishments are known for their meticulous attention to detail, exceptional service, and the use of the finest ingredients.

- **Benu:** A celebrated restaurant by Chef Corey Lee, Benu has maintained its three Michelin stars for many years. Known for its elegant, minimalist ambiance and innovative dishes, it's a must-visit for those seeking a unique culinary experience.
- **Atelier Crenn:** This three Michelin-starred restaurant, led by Chef Dominique Crenn, offers a poetic approach to modern French cuisine. Chef Crenn's creative and artistic presentations make dining at Atelier Crenn a truly memorable experience.
- **Quince:** Located in Jackson Square, Chef Michael Tusk's Quince features a tasting menu that showcases the best local and seasonal ingredients. The restaurant's warm, sophisticated atmosphere adds to the exceptional dining experience.

Internationally Inspired Fine Dining

San Francisco's fine dining scene also includes a variety of internationally inspired restaurants that bring global flavors to the city.

- **Saison:** This three Michelin-starred restaurant by Chef Joshua Skenes offers a seasonal, ingredient-driven menu that emphasizes open-fire cooking. Saison's intimate setting and meticulous craftsmanship have made it one of the top dining destinations in the city.
- **Acquerello:** Chef Suzette Gresham's Acquerello is a two Michelin-starred Italian restaurant known for its refined dishes and elegant ambiance. The restaurant's commitment to traditional Italian techniques combined with modern touches has earned it numerous accolades.
- **Campton Place:** Situated in the Taj Campton Place hotel, Chef Srijith Gopinathan's restaurant blends Indian and Californian flavors in an innovative and sophisticated menu. The restaurant's innovative dishes and luxurious atmosphere have earned it two Michelin stars.

San Francisco's fine dining establishments provide an exceptional culinary experience that reflects the city's diverse culture and innovative spirit. Whether you're indulging in a multi-course tasting menu or exploring globally inspired dishes, San Francisco's fine dining scene offers unforgettable experiences for food enthusiasts.

Casual Eateries

San Francisco's casual eateries offer a more relaxed dining experience without compromising on quality. From neighborhood bistros to trendy cafes, these establishments provide a diverse range of delicious and affordable options.

- Neighborhood Favorites

Casual eateries are often neighborhood institutions, beloved by locals for their cozy ambiance and consistently good food.

- **Zazie:** Located in Cole Valley, Zazie is a charming French bistro known for its brunch offerings and welcoming atmosphere. Popular dishes include the gingerbread pancakes and the eggs benedict.
- **Tony's Pizza Napoletana:** This North Beach hotspot is famous for its award-winning pizzas and laid-back vibe. The menu also features a variety of Italian dishes and creative small plates.
- **Foreign Cinema:** A Mission District favorite, Foreign Cinema combines a unique dining experience with a menu of Californian-Mediterranean dishes like lavender fried chicken and slow-cooked pork shoulder. Its outdoor courtyard with a nightly film screening adds to its charm.

Trendy Cafes and Diners

San Francisco is also home to a plethora of trendy cafes and diners that serve up everything from classic American fare to innovative brunch dishes.

- **Tartine Bakery:** Located in the Mission District, Tartine Bakery is renowned for its freshly baked bread and pastries. The morning bun and croque monsieur are standout items.
- **Mama's on Washington Square:** A beloved cafe in North Beach, Mama's offers hearty breakfast and lunch options, including their famous eggs benedict and cinnamon brioche French toast.
- **Plow:** This Potrero Hill diner draws crowds for its all-day breakfast and comfort food offerings. The lemon ricotta pancakes and the Plow platter, featuring eggs, potatoes, and sausage, are must-try dishes.

San Francisco's casual eateries provide a relaxed and enjoyable dining experience, showcasing the city's diverse culinary scene. Whether you're indulging in a leisurely brunch or savoring a slice of artisanal pizza, these establishments offer something for everyone.

Street Food and Food Trucks

San Francisco's street food and food truck scene is vibrant and diverse, offering a quick and delicious way to sample a wide range of cuisines. From taco stands to gourmet food trucks, these mobile eateries are an integral part of the city's culinary landscape.

Classic Street Food

The city's classic street food vendors have become iconic symbols of San Francisco's eclectic lifestyle. In addition to the already mentioned dishes, street carts in the city offer:

- **Tamales:** Often sold from carts or small vendors, these traditional Mexican treats are popular for their savory fillings and delicious masa dough.
- **Roasted Chestnuts:** Especially popular during the colder months, roasted chestnuts are a warm, fragrant snack sold by street vendors in busy areas like Union Square.
- **Bacon-Wrapped Hot Dogs:** These flavorful hot dogs, often topped with grilled onions and peppers, are a staple of San Francisco's street food scene, particularly in the Mission District.

Gourmet Food Trucks

San Francisco's food truck scene has exploded in recent years, with gourmet trucks offering inventive and high-quality dishes from around the world.

- **Senor Sisig:** This food truck combines Filipino and Mexican flavors, serving up delicious dishes like sisig burritos, tacos, and loaded fries.
- **The Chairman:** Known for its mouthwatering steamed and baked buns, The Chairman offers a variety of fillings such as pork belly, miso tofu, and Coca-Cola braised pork.
- **Curry Up Now:** This popular food truck brings Indian street food to the streets of San Francisco, with items like tikka masala

burritos, deconstructed samosas, and sexy fries (sweet potato fries topped with cheese and curry).

Pop-Up Markets

In addition to individual food trucks, San Francisco hosts several pop-up markets where multiple vendors gather to offer a variety of street food options.

- **Off the Grid:** This mobile food market features a rotating lineup of food trucks and vendors at various locations throughout the city. It's a great place to try a diverse range of cuisines in one spot.
- **Ferry Plaza Farmers Market:** Held at the Ferry Building, this market not only offers fresh produce but also a variety of food vendors selling everything from artisanal cheeses to gourmet sandwiches.
- **SoMa StrEat Food Park:** This permanent food truck park in the SoMa neighborhood features a rotating selection of food trucks and a lively atmosphere with picnic tables and entertainment.

Whether you're craving a quick snack or a gourmet meal on the go, San Francisco's street food and food truck scene has something to satisfy every palate. These mobile eateries offer a convenient and delicious way to experience the city's diverse culinary offerings.

Ethnic Cuisine

San Francisco is a global melting pot, and nowhere is this more evident than in its diverse neighborhoods, each offering a rich tapestry of ethnic cuisines. North Beach, Chinatown, and the Mission District are three of the most vibrant areas, where visitors can indulge in authentic and delicious foods from around the world.

North Beach

North Beach, located in the northeastern part of San Francisco, is a historic neighborhood that celebrates the legacy of Italian immigrants who settled in the city in the late 19th and early 20th centuries. Though the area has evolved over the years, it retains its charming, old-world ambiance and remains a culinary haven for lovers of Italian cuisine.

Columbus Avenue, the heart of North Beach, is lined with Italian restaurants, cafes, and bakeries that serve classic dishes such as pasta, pizza, and cannoli. Notable establishments include Tony's Pizza Napoletana, known for its award-winning Neapolitan pizzas, where visitors can savor a slice of history along with their pie. For a sweet treat, Stella Pastry & Cafe, founded in 1942, offers a delightful selection of Italian pastries, cannoli, and espresso.

The neighborhood is also famous for its annual Italian Heritage Parade, held in October to celebrate Columbus Day. The parade features floats, marching bands, and cultural performances, attracting visitors from around the world. During the celebration, Columbus Avenue transforms into a lively celebration of Italian culture and cuisine, with vendors selling sausage and peppers, arancini, and other Italian street foods.

Chinatown

San Francisco's Chinatown, one of the largest and oldest Chinatowns in the United States, was established by Chinese immigrants in the mid-19th century. The neighborhood is a bustling enclave that offers a wide array of authentic Chinese cuisine.

Chinatown's streets are filled with markets, bakeries, and restaurants that showcase the diverse flavors of China. Dim sum, a traditional Cantonese meal of small plates, is a popular choice, with restaurants like City View and Good Mong Kok Bakery offering a variety of dumplings, buns, and other delicacies served from rolling carts. For a more casual bite, Z & Y Restaurant is famous for its spicy Sichuan dishes, a must-try for any visitor.

In addition to Cantonese and Sichuan cuisine, Chinatown also offers dishes from other regions of China. House of Nanking serves innovative takes on traditional dishes, while Sam Wo Restaurant is known for its comforting bowls of wonton soup and BBQ pork rolls.

Chinatown's vibrant food scene is complemented by its lively street markets, where vendors sell fresh produce, seafood, and exotic ingredients. These markets provide a glimpse into the neighborhood's rich culinary traditions and are a must-visit for any food enthusiast.

Mission District

The Mission District, located in the southeastern part of San Francisco, is a vibrant neighborhood known for its Mexican and Latin American cuisine. Often referred to as "the Mission," this area offers an immersive experience of Latin culture and cuisine.

The Mission District is renowned for its taquerias, where diners can enjoy authentic Mexican dishes. Popular spots include La Taqueria, famous for its Mission-style burritos, and Taqueria El Farolito, where guests can enjoy a variety of tacos, burritos, and quesadillas filled with flavorful meats and fresh ingredients.

For those seeking traditional Latin American dishes, the Mission offers a variety of options. Poc-Chuc is known for its Yucatecan cuisine, including dishes like cochinita pibil (slow-roasted pork) and poc chuc (grilled pork). Puerto Alegre serves classic Mexican dishes like enchiladas and chile rellenos in a festive atmosphere.

The Mission District's food scene extends beyond savory dishes to include an array of sweet treats and beverages. La Palma Mexicatessen offers freshly made tortillas and Mexican pastries, while St. Francis Fountain, a nostalgic soda fountain, serves classic American and Mexican desserts. For a refreshing treat, visitors can try paletas (Mexican popsicles) at Casa de Paletas.

In addition to its culinary delights, the Mission District is known for its vibrant street art and cultural festivals. The annual Carnaval San Francisco, held in May, features colorful parades, live music, and dance performances, celebrating Latin American and Caribbean cultures.

North Beach, Chinatown, and the Mission District each provide a unique culinary journey, showcasing the rich traditions and flavors of their respective cultures. Exploring these neighborhoods offers a delicious and immersive experience of San Francisco's diverse food scene.

Food Markets

San Francisco is renowned for its diverse culinary landscape, and its food markets are some of the best places to experience this gastronomic variety. Among these, the Ferry Building Marketplace and Off the Grid stand out as must-visit destinations for food lovers seeking a wide array of flavors and culinary delights.

Ferry Building Marketplace

Located at the foot of Market Street along the Embarcadero, the Ferry Building Marketplace is one of San Francisco's most iconic indoor food markets. Housed in a historic ferry terminal, the market retains much of its architectural charm with arched windows, high ceilings, and a bustling, lively atmosphere.

The Ferry Building Marketplace is a food lover's paradise, offering an eclectic mix of vendors that cater to a wide range of tastes and preferences. Visitors can find everything from artisanal cheese and fresh oysters to gourmet chocolates and exotic spices. Popular vendors include Hog Island Oyster Co., known for its fresh oysters and seafood offerings, and Acme Bread Company, famous for its artisanal bread.

In addition to its food stalls, the Ferry Building features several sit-down restaurants where visitors can enjoy a full meal. The Slanted Door offers a menu focused on modern Vietnamese cuisine, while Boulette's Larder serves up farm-to-table dishes with a focus on local ingredients. The market also houses retail shops selling kitchenware, specialty foods, and unique gifts, making it a one-stop destination for both culinary delights and shopping.

Off the Grid

Off the Grid, often referred to as a mobile food extravaganza, is an open-air food market that showcases some of the best food trucks and street food vendors in San Francisco. Founded in 2010, Off the Grid has become a beloved weekly tradition, drawing thousands of visitors to its various locations around the city.

The market operates year-round, with its flagship event held on Friday evenings at Fort Mason Center. Off the Grid features over 30 local vendors offering an incredible variety of dishes, from classic comfort foods to innovative culinary creations. Notable vendors include Señor Sisig, known for its Filipino fusion tacos and burritos, and The Chairman, famous for its steamed and baked buns.

One of the highlights of Off the Grid is the opportunity to sample a diverse array of international cuisines all in one place. Visitors can enjoy everything from Korean BBQ and Indian curries to Peruvian ceviche and Italian gelato. The market's lively atmosphere, combined with its scenic waterfront locations, makes it a perfect spot for a leisurely outing with friends and family.

Both the Ferry Building Marketplace and Off the Grid offer unique and memorable culinary experiences, showcasing the best of San Francisco's vibrant food scene. Whether you're exploring the historic indoor market of the Ferry Building or indulging in the diverse street food offerings at Off the Grid, these food markets are essential destinations for any food enthusiast visiting the city.

Made in United States
Troutdale, OR
03/14/2025